THE JOURNAL JURISPRUDENCE

VOLUME ELEVEN

"LOOKING FORWARD"

Contributors: Christoph Bezemek
Vienna University of Economics and Business

Lutz-Christian Wolff
The Chinese University of Hong Kong

John A. Bruegger
Washington University in St. Louis

Editor: Aron Ping D'Souza
University of Melbourne

MICHAELMAS TERM
OCTOBER 2011

Elias Clark

PUBLISHED BY THE ELIAS CLARK GROUP

DISTRIBUTED IN CONNECTION WITH THE GALE GROUP,
A PART OF CENGAGE LEARNING

The Elias Clark Group
www.elias-clark.com

GPO Box 5001
Melbourne, Victoria 3001
Australia

First Published 2010.

Cataloguing-in-Publication entry

Editor:	D'Souza, Aron Ping.
Authors:	D'Souza, Aron Ping. Bezemek, Christoph. Wolff, Lutz-Christian. Bruegger, John A.
Title:	The Journal Jurisprudence, Volume Eleven, "Looking Forward."
ISBN:	978-0-9871170-2-1 (pbk.)
ISSN:	1836-0955
Subjects:	Law – jurisprudence. Philosophy –general.

This edition may be cited as

(2011) J. Juris.

followed by the page number

ABOUT THE TYPEFACE

The Journal Jurisprudence is typeset in Garamond 12 and the footnotes are set in Garamond 10. The typeface was named for Claude Garamond (c. 1480 - 1561) and are based on the work of Jean Jannon. By 1540, Garamond became a popular choice in the books of the French imperial court, particularly under King Francis I. Garamond was said to be based on the handwriting of Angelo Vergecio, a librarian to the King. The italics of Garamond are credited to Robert Grandjon, an assistant to Claude Garamond. The font was re-popularised in the art deco era and became a mainstay on twentieth-century publication. In the 1970s, the font was redesigned by the International Typeface Corporation, which forms the basis of the variant of Garamond used in this Journal.

TABLE OF CONTENTS

CALL FOR PAPERS

The field of jurisprudence lies at the nexus of law and politics, the practical and the philosophical. By understanding the theoretical foundations of law, jurisprudence can inform us of the place of legal structures within larger philosophical frameworks. In its inaugural edition, *The Journal Jurisprudence* received many creative and telling answers to the question, "What is Law?" For the second edition, the editors challenged the scholarly and lay communities to inquire into intersection between jurisprudence and economics.

With the backing of our diverse and disparate community, *The Journal Jurisprudence* has now evolved into a more diverse form. We will no longer be setting a question for each issue, but instead designing issues around the articles we received. Therefore, we invite scholars, lawyers, judges, philosophers and lay people tackle the any and all of the great questions of law. Knowing that ideas come in all forms, papers can be of any length, although emphasis is placed on readability by lay audiences.

Papers may engage with case studies, philosophical arguments or any other method that answers philosophical question applicable to the law. Importantly, articles will be selected based upon quality and the readability of works by non-specialists. The intent of the Journal is to involve non-scholars in the important debates of legal philosophy.

The Journal also welcomes and encourages submissions of articles typically not found in law journals, including opinionated or personalised insights into the philosophy of law and its applications to practical situations.

Jurisprudence is published four times per year, to coincide with the four terms of the legal year, in an attractive paperback and electronic edition.

All authors who submit to this edition will be provided with a complementary copy of the journal.

Length: Any length is acceptable, although readability to non-specialist is key.

Presentation Style: Papers must comply with the Australian Guide to Legal Citations, Second Edition published by the Melbourne University Law Review. An electronic edition is available at, http://mulr.law.unimelb.edu.au/PDFs/aglc_dl.pdf

Submission: You must submit electronically in Microsoft Word format to editor@jurisprudence.com.au. Extraneous formatting is discouraged.

Correspondence can also be sent to this address. If you are considering submitting an article, you are invited to contact the editor to discuss ideas before authoring a work.

SUBSCRIPTION INFORMATION

The Journal is published four times per year in an attractive softcover book. Subscription to the Journal can be achieved by two methods:

1) Single issues can be purchased on amazon.com. Our publishers, the Elias Clark Group, set a retail price for each edition, typically AU$40. However, due to their agreement with amazon.com, the price may vary for retail customers.

2) A subscription to the Journal can be purchased for AU$150 per year, or AU$280 for two years. This price includes postage throughout the world. Payment can be made by international bank cheque, but not a personal cheque, to:

   The Journal Jurisprudence,
   C/o The Elias Clark Group
   GPO Box 5001
   Melbourne, Victoria, Australia.

Alternatively, the Journal is available online at www.jurisprudence.com.au and can be read there free of charge.

EDITORIAL: LOOKING FORWARD

Being an Oxonian, I chose to adopt the Oxford names for the terms of the year to denote our quarterly issue. Michaelmas coincides with the start of the academic year and, for the courts of England and the United States, the start of the legal year. Not just across the pond does the name unify legal traditions, Michaelmas is also the only term name used by both Oxford and Cambridge. The Supreme Court of the United States does not adopt the name for its autumn term but it does, by no coincidence, begin its legal year on the first Monday of October, which is often the feast of St Michael and All Angels. I was recently told that even some American law schools adopt the Oxonian trilogy of terms, Michaelmas, Hilary and Trinity.[1]

For *The Journal Jurisprudence*, October and Michaelmas is also the start of a new year for us. Now into our fourth year, the Journal grows with each day and astounded me with its reach. I was proud to find a copy an early issues in a used book store in Melbourne some weeks ago, diligently underlined by what I imagine to be a young scholar. There are cycles to the legal year and cycles to legal knowledge, and I hope that this issue will be highlighted and scribbled upon for years to come.

Jurisprudence has, unlike many fields, a generally unified history. Although one could point to the many camps of scholars, from Hart in England to Posner in Chicago and Stone in Sydney, there has always been an exchange of ideas in the

[1] E.g., http://www.cooley.edu/prospective/calendar.html

recent history of legal philosophy. Although early jurisprudential scholars were far away geographically, international collaborations and the coincidental dawn of high speed communication brought them together. Therefore, I can say with confidence that legal philosophy shares one history and together we look forward to a bright future.

We are pleased to show how international collaborations can ensure the future of jurisprudence. This issue contains articles from three distinguished scholars from different parts of the world and shows both the intellectual and theoretical diversity of legal philosophy in the modern age.

Aron Ping D'Souza
Editor
7 October 2011
Melbourne, Australia

CONSTITUTIONAL CORE(S): AMENDMENTS, ENTRENCHMENTS, ETERNITIES AND BEYOND PROLEGOMENA TO A THEORY OF NORMATIVE VOLATILITY

Christoph Bezemek[*]

Preliminary Remarks

This essay is not an exhaustive disquisition on the topic. It is not meant to be. It is an agglomeration of thoughts, raising questions rather than providing answers, a sketch rather than an elaborated concept; a possible starting point for a broader and more detailed discussion.

I. *Introduction: Constitutional Persistence – Constitutional Flux*

A. **Heraclitus and Plato (I)**

The concept of a constitution is inseparably connected with the idea of persistence. Constitutions are to provide a solid framework for political action:[1] While (the perception of) factual phenomena and accordingly their normative appreciation are constantly changing, constitutions are deemed to serve as foundation for the manner (as well as the extent to which) these phenomena are addressed. Thus, constitutions depend on inherent stability; an exclusively 'Heraclitian' conception of dynamic constitutions in constant normative flux

[*] Assistant Professor of Law, Institute of Austrian and European Public Law, Vienna University of Economics and Business (WU).

As usual friends and colleagues gave advice that made a (somewhat) coherent piece out of this essay. The arguments presented substantially benefited from the critique they all generously contributed – which is, however, not to say that all of them would agree to what is written on the following pages. In particular I would like to thank Claudia Fuchs, Georg Lienbacher, Michael Potacs, Andreas Th. Müller and, of course, Michael Holoubek for their invaluable support. I am also indebted to the participants of the IOER faculty workshop and the participants at the International Conference on Constitutional Pluralism at the West Bengal National University of Juridical Sciences in Kolkata in Nov 2010 where parts of this paper were presented. Mihir Chatterjee improved the writing style dramatically. Finally, without Matthias Lukan's admirable research skills this article would not have been written in the first place. Errors, inaccuracies, and the like, however, remain mine.

[1] *See* Werner Kägi, *Die Verfassung als rechtliche Grundordnung des Staates* (Reprint 1971) 51.

would not meet these requirements: 'A government, forever changing and changeable, is, indeed, in a state bordering upon anarchy and confusion'.[2]

Still the framework's design has to ensure a sufficient capacity to respond to social reality. As much as constitutions serve as normative foundations of political systems elevated from normal politics, they cannot elude completely from being reactive to a changing political environment.[3] Otherwise their requirements would turn out to become a normative corset too tight to regulate political practice reasonably any longer. Thus, also a 'Platonic' vision of a static constitution trying to establish normative truth, will not prove to be sufficiently workable:[4] 'A government, which, in its own organization, provides no means of change, but assumes to be fixed and unalterable, must, after a while, become wholly unsuited to the circumstances of the nation; and it will either degenerate into a despotism, or by the pressure of its inequalities bring on a revolution.'[5]

A balance has to be struck between dynamic elements providing for the system's flexibility and static elements providing for the system's persistence in order to safeguard its functionality. 'That useful alterations will be suggested by experience, [can] not but be foreseen'.[6] A 'healing principle' is to be introduced;[7] as '[i]t is wise [...] in every government, and especially in a republic, to provide means for altering, and improving the fabric of government, as time and experience, or the new phases of human affairs, may render proper, to promote the happiness and safety of the people. The great principle to be sought is to make the changes practicable, but not too easy.'[8]

This essay is dedicated to the quest of this principle.

---

[2] Joseph Story, *Commentaries on the Constitution of the United States* III (1833) Ch XLI § 1821.

[3] *Cf* Wahl, 'Verfassunggebung – Verfassungsänderung – Verfassungswandel' I in Wahl (ed), *Verfassungsänderung, Verfassungswandel, Verfassungsinterpretation* (2008) 29, 30.

[4] *See* e.g. Dreier, *Grundgesetz* (Second Edition 2004) Art 79 Abs 2 at 11; Grimm, 'Verfassungsfunktion und Grundgesetzreform' 97 *Archiv des öffentlichen Rechts* 489 (505).

[5] Story, above n 2, Ch XLI § 1821.

[6] James Madison, *Federalist* No 43 No. 43 (1788) – edited by Jacob E. Cooke (1961).

[7] Thomas Pownall quoted according to Wood, *The Creation of the American Republic 1776-1787* (Reprint 1998) 613.

[8] Story, above n 2 Ch XLI § 1821.

B. Constitutive Laws – Constitutional Law

I will distinguish between a *dis*-positive and a *positive* approach to the conception of a constitution. This distinction is based on the question whether or not formal attributes grant additional stability to some legal norms while denying it to others:

A legal system may lack any formal distinction between its various legal provisions, leaving it to the *dis*-posal of a certain body (legislator in a broader sense) to alter them all likewise. This legal system does not grant any additional formal stability to norms considered to be of fundamental importance (*constitutive* laws), in comparison to ordinary legislation dealing with questions concerning normal politics. Due to this lack of distinction between ordinary legislation and *constitutive* laws, the latter remain open to alteration by regular means – an inherently dynamic conception.

Legal systems may, however, decrease this dynamic on a formal level by *positively* stating additional requirements to be met for the alteration of certain provisions; thus creating a sphere of *constitutional* law.

C. Heraclitus and Plato (II)

A comparison between legal systems guided by a substantive concept of *constitutive* laws and legal systems structured according to formalized conceptions positively creating *constitutional* laws seems to be a reasonable starting point to walk along the path that leads from the 'Heraclitian' perception of normative flux to a 'Platonic' vision of normative truth referred to above.

Having sketched the difference between the two concepts, I will focus on various modes of normative stabilization legal systems provide by distinguishing *constitutional* laws from ordinary legislation by the means of specified requirements to be met to amend or revise *constitutional* law. I will then introduce a multi-tier structure distinguishing different degrees of *constitutional* amendment within legal systems, eventually outlining a model of positive stabilization. This model will draw our attention to doctrinal, sociological and theoretical questions.[9]

---

[9] Intellectual honesty demands to add other aspects, in particular on a political and on an interpretative level (*Verfassungswandlung* – see, for example, Jellinek, *Verfassungsänderung und Verfassungswandlung* (Reprint 1996); Böckenförde, 'Anmerkungen zum Begriff Verfassungswandel' in *Festschrift Lerche* (1993) 3; Wahl, 'Verfassunggebung – Verfassungsänderung – Verfassungswandel II' in Wahl (ed), *Verfassungsänderung,*

D. Beyond Dualism?

Finally I will address the question whether, and to what extent, boundaries are set to positive stabilization, finding a possible affirmative answer on a pre-positive level by introducing a structural principle based on social contract theory. This answer – while at first glance leading 'Beyond Dualism' – in essence, will turn out to stay attached to the participatory principle underlying a dualist model of constitutional law.

II. The **dis**-*positive Perspective*

A. A Substantive Perception

''With us,'' Albert Venn Dicey stated in 1902 'laws […] are called constitutional because they refer to subjects supposed to affect the fundamental institutions of the state, and not because they are legally more sacred or difficult to change than other laws';[10] an astonishing statement when assessed from the point of view of contemporary continental European law: Dicey's perspective refers to the constitution first and foremost by its claim to provide an answer to the fundamental questions of how the state is structured, of how community and individual define their relation to each other.

This approach is based on a substantive perception of legal provisions constitutive for the community (*constitutive* laws), a purely substantive perception, refraining from positively creating an elevated sphere of *constitutional* law beyond normal politics: 'Parliament of today cannot fetter the Parliament of tomorrow with any sort of permanent restraints, so that entrenched

---

Verfassungswandel, Verfassungsinterpretation (2008) 65; Voßkuhle, 'Gibt es und Wozu nutzt eine Lehre vom Verfassungswandel?' in Wahl (ed), *Verfassungsänderung, Verfassungswandel, Verfassungsinterpretation* (2008) 201; Schulze-Fielitz, 'Verfassung als Prozess von Verfassungsänderungen ohne Verfassungstextänderungen' in Wahl (Ed), *Verfassungänderung, Verfassungswandel, Verfassungsinterpretation* (2008) 219; Barak, *The Judge in a Democracy* (2008) 130; Mc Ginnis/Rappaport, 'Our Our Supermajoritarian Constitution' (2002) 80 Texas Law Review 703, 802) but also with regard to the influence specific techniques or formal requirements (as, for example, Incorporation-Clauses – *see*, i.a., Wiederin, 'Über Inkorporationsgebote und andere Strategien zur Sicherung der Einheit der Verfassung' [2004] *Zeitschrift für öffentliches Recht* 175) may have on a constitution's relative rigidity that are not covered by this essay.
The capacity of the model introduced below, however, will not be exhausted by the rather formal focus of the questions I try to address predominantly in this paper. For a recent enquiry of the topic based on a quite different approach – *see* the interesting study of Elkins et al, *The Endurance of National Constitutions* (2009).

[10] Albert Venn Dicey, *Introduction to the Study of the Law of the Constitution* (Reprint 2005) 123.

provisions are impossible. That, at any rate, appears to be the view of the legal establishment'.[11]

While certain norms define the state's very nature substantively they do not enjoy elevated normative authority in terms of procedural requirements; there is no constrain to 'the right of the Crown and the two Houses to modify or repeal any law whatever; they can alter the succession to the Crown or repeal the Acts of Union in the same manner in which they can pass an Act enabling a company to make a new railway from Oxford to London':[12] formally, *constitutive* laws remain at the legislator's *dis*-posal.

B. Flexible Constitutions – Normative Dynamic

This lack of formal restrain, Parliament's capacity to alter any law 'without special procedure, and by simple Act, [...] however fundamental it may seem to be',[13] prompted Dicey's contemporary James Bryce to define constitutions as the English as flexible 'because they have elasticity, because they can be bent and altered in form'.[14]

Assessed from the perspective of formal stabilization such *flexible constitutions* allow for a great extent of normative dynamic.

This is, of course, not to say that the constitution lacks normative relevance in legal systems following a *dis*-positive approach: Also a substantive perception implicates increased stability when compared to ordinary legislation dealing with normal politics simply by introducing such a distinction to the relevant discourse;[15] thereby granting special status to the laws that may be considered being part of a community's foundation.[16,17]

---

[11] *See* HWR Wade, *Constitutional Fundamentals*, 32nd Hamlyn Lectures (1980). It has to be highlighted, however, that this view is not undisputed – *cf.* e.g. for the 'new approach' to Supremacy Ivor Jennings, The Law and the Constitution, (5th ed 1959) 152 and Michael Gordon, 'The Conceptual Foundations of Parliamentary Sovereignty: Reconsidering Jennings and Wade' (2009) Public Law 519 supporting Jennings' position.

[12] Dicey, above n 10, 122-123.

[13] Philip Seaforth James, *Introduction to English Law* (12th ed 1989) 118.

[14] James Bryce, *Studies in History and Jurisprudence* Vol I (Reprint 2005) 154.

[15] Setting aside Parliament's Sovereignty itself as link to an assumption of a hierarchical and thus comparatively static (*cf* Christian Starck, *Verfassungen* [2009] 385) structure of the United Kingdom's legal system – *see* e.g. Jeffrey Goldsworthy, 'Abdicating and limiting Parliament's Sovereignty' (2006) 17 *KC LJ* 255, 261.

[16] For further developments in the relationship between parliament and the judiciary *cf* CJS Knight, 'Bi-Polar Sovereignty restated' (2009) *Cambridge Law Journal* 361.

The *dis*-positive approach, however, grants such additional stability on a political level only and does not provide for an exact guideline that would help us to define how (i.e. by which specific acts and provisions) a country's constitution is composed.[18]

Consequently substance precedes form when following the *dis*-positive approach;[19] substance exclusively defines the status a legal provision qualifies to claim.

III. The positive perspective

C. Stabilization by Formalization

Retaining Bryce's classification, 'rigid' constitutions mark the counterpart to the flexible structures based on the *dis*-positive concept I referred to above. Far from easily being 'bent and altered', rigid constitutions are 'hard and fixed'.[20]

What Marshall stated famously in *Marbury v. Madison* is overall true for the structure of 'rigid' constitutions according to Bryce: They have to be regarded as a 'superior, paramount law, unchangeable by ordinary means'.[21] By drawing 'formal and technical distinctions between laws of different kinds',[22] this conception by its very nature positively shifts the constitution's structure towards an increasingly static design: Irrespective of the techniques used,[23] the

[17] This question has become even more important, when the Human Rights Act 1998 was introduced providing for a special procedure with regard to the compliance of a proposed statute with human rights. *See*, e.g., KD Ewing, 'The Human Rights Act and Parliamentary Democracy' 62 *Mod. L. Rev.* 79 or Julian Rivers, 'Menschenrechtsschutz im Vereinigten Königreich' (2001) *Juristenzeitung* 127, 130.
For the relation between Acts of Parliament and European Union Law *cf.* R *v Secretary of State for Transport ex p. Factortame* (no. 1) [1990] 2 AC 85; R *v Secretary of State for Transport ex p. Factortame* (no. 2) [1991] 1 AC 603.

[18] *See* Dicey, above n 10, cxlv-cxlvi. For the continental-european perspective *see* Hans Kelsen, *Die Verfassungsgesetze der Republik Deutsch-Österreich* Vol III (1919) 112. For the problems arising in this context *see* Christoph Bezemek, 'Die Rolle des Bundespräsidenten im Gesetzgebungsverfahren' in Georg Lienbacher, Gerhard Wielinger (eds), *Jahrbuch öffentliches Recht* (2009) 89, 94-95. *See* also Georg Jellinek's critical assessment: *Allgemeine Staatslehre* (3rd ed Reprint 1960) 533.

[19] *L'essence précède l'existence* one may add – *cf.* Jean Paul Sartre, *L'Existentialisme est un Humanisme* (Gallimard 1996) 27.

[20] Bryce, above n 14, 154.

[21] Marbury v. Madison 5 U.S. 177 (1803).

[22] Bryce, above n 14 155.

[23] I will distinguish ordinary legislation and *constitutional* amendment with regard to their comparatively dynamic or comparatively static character notwithstanding the fact that, of course, there are differences between the paths chosen for *constitutional* amendment in particular with regard to the question whether *constitutional* amendment basically originates in- or outside

positive elevation of certain laws compared to the normal politics passed into law by ordinary legislation provides additional stability for laws enjoying *constitutional* status.

D. Creating *constitutional* law

But form not only precedes substance in the positive approach to constitutions;[24] form not only *defines* the normative status a legal provision qualifies to claim:[25] As a constitution's amendment procedure states the requirements to alter certain legal provisions it serves not only as yardstick whether or not requirements have been met, providing an additional rule of change.[26] Additionally, it is the formalized procedure that introduces the distinction between ordinary (future) legislation and *constitutional* law in the first place.[27]The introduction of a (second) rule of change, asking for elevated requirements to be met for the enactment and alteration of provisions vested with elevated formal authority not only upholds but also recognizes and thus creates *constitutional* laws; a quite remarkable fact...

E. *Constitutive* vs *constitutional* laws

1) Foundations

But which laws should enter this newly established sphere?[28] At first glance the answer is obvious: the *constitutive* laws referred to above, in order to grant additional formal stability to these fundamental provisions;[29] comforting the demand for stability when it comes to the state's foundation.[30] With this approach of granting additional stability to certain legal provisions by the means of formal requirements the constitution seems secured from a random

---

the legislative power. *See* drastically for first instance Article 76 of the Weimar Constitution and compare for example the mechanism for *constitutional* amendment according to Article V of the US Constitution.

24 Again: Sartre, above n 19, 26: *l'existence précède l'essence.*

25 With similar conclusions Friedrich Müller, *Fragment (über) die verfassungsgebende Gewalt des Volkes* (1995) 37.

26 *Cf.* H.L.A. Hart, *The Concept of Law* (1972) 93.

27 For the transition from a dispositive perception to a positive conception exemplified by the Austrian Constitution *see* Hans Kelsen, *Die Verfassungsgesetze der Republik Deutsch-Österreich* Vol I (1919) 90 and Kelsen, above n 18, 112.

28 For a functional approach to this question in more recent scholarship *see*, for example, Ruth Gavison, 'What belongs in a Constitution?' (2002) 13 Constitutional Political Economy 89, 91-94.

29 *See* i.a. Hans Kelsen, 'Wesen und Entwicklung der Staatsgerichtsbarkeit' (Reprint) in Koja (Ed), *Hans Kelsen oder die Reine Rechtslehre* (1988) 113.

30 Hans Kelsen, *Allgemeine Staatslehre* (1925) 252.

majority's volition.[31] Formally recognized *constitutional* laws in this regard may thus be described as minority-protective,[32] evening out the problem that has been referred to by de Tocqueville as 'Tyranny of the Majority';[33] insulating *constitutional* law 'from the absolutism of majority will' by protecting it against acts that do not enjoy the same enlarged extent of political legitimacy as *constitutional* provisions.[34]

Many questions may be raised against the backdrop of these observations:

– Do these characteristics stand in tension with the idea of liberty or rather promote it?[35]

– To what extent does such formal normative stability actually aim to be an approximation to 'truth' on a normative level?[36]

– Whether and to what extent may such a 'minority-protective' effect,[37] turn into a 'tyranny of the minority'?[38]

---

[31] Jellinek, above n 18, 534.

[32] Kelsen, above n 30, 252. Similarly Bryce, above 14, 201 distinguishes four different motives for establishing constitutions guided by the idea of formal distinction to ordinary legislation:

'1) The desire of the citizens, that is to say, of the part of the population which enjoys political rights, to secure their own rights when threatened, and to restrain the action of their ruler or rulers.

(2) The desire of the citizens, or of a ruler who wishes to please the citizens, to set out the form of the preexisting system of government in definite and positive terms precluding further controversy regarding it.

(3) The desire of those who are erecting a new political community to embody the scheme of polity under which they propose to be governed, in an instrument which shall secure its permanence and make it comprehensible by the people.

(4) The desire of separate communities, or of distinct groups or sections within a large (and probably loosely united) community, to settle and set forth the terms under which their respective rights and interests are to be safe-guarded, and effective joint action in common matters secured, through one government.'

One may have to discuss to what extent these categories still prove to be valid today.

[33] Alexis de Tocqueville, *Demokratie in Amerika* (Reprint 1950) 39. *Cf* also and in particular John Stuart Mill, *On Liberty* Ch I and James Madison, *Federalist* No 51 edited by Jacob E. Cooke (1961).

[34] Bruce Ackerman, *We the People: Foundations* (1993) 264.

[35] Hans Kelsen, *Vom Wesen und Wert der Demokratie* (Reprint 1963) 8-9.

[36] *See*, for example, Carl Schmitt, *Die geistesgeschichtliche Lage des heutigen Parlamentarismus* (3rd ed 1926) 36-7 referring to the problem of defining a people's true will irrespective of the majority's volition; granting additional stability to certain legal provisions by the means of formal requirements addresses this problem by fortifying the provision's *Geltungsanspruch* (*see* Jürgen Habermas, 'Wahrheitstheorien' in Fahrenbach (ed), *Wirklichkeit und Reflexion* [1973] 211, 218) in a formal manner.

[37] The effects, of course, vary depending on the specific design; *cf*, in particular, Ackerman's model of a 'supermajoritarian-escalator' increasingly strengthening the minority's position – Bruce Ackerman, *Before the next Attack:* (2006) 80 and, most recently, *Decline and Fall of the American Republic* (2010) 168.

– Does it rather preserve the *status quo* or prevent an undesirable subjection under a random majority's volition?[39]

2) Detachment

This ideal-type description, however, is just one side of what may come along with the formal creation of a sphere of *constitutional* law. Giving it closer scrutiny this approach consequently also causes detachment of the formally elevated laws from the idea inherent to a substantive conception of *constitutive* laws as described above, subsequently creating the fundamental character attributed to a legal provision by granting it elevated status.[40] From this perspective, any content may become *constitutional* law. And many examples show that the creation of *constitutional* law does not have to be in pursuance of a noble goal or guided by the intention of regulating the community's fundamental concerns.[41] Form and function fall apart.

On the one hand this formal creation of a *constitutional* sphere provides a much greater extent of clarity when it comes to define what a community's constitution *is* when compared to the inductive approach deriving from the substantive conception of *constitutive* laws. However, the positive approach does not provide us with immanent criteria to assess what these *constitutional* laws *ought* to be. *Constitutional* laws may lawfully be enacted in order to avoid judicial review of laws which, if regularly enacted, would be considered un*constitutional*,

---

[38] *See*, for the American Constitution, Sanford Levinson, *Our undemocratic Constitution* (2006) 204. For the minority-protective effect the amendment procedure of the Articles of the Confederation yielded *see* James Madison, *Federalist* No 40, (1788) – edited by Jacob E. Cooke (1961) 263. Also *see* the way Hamilton perceives the minority-protective effect of supermajorities – *Federalist* 58, (1788) – edited by Jacob E. Cooke (1961) 396.

[39] *See*, for example, Schaller, Consent for Change: Article V and the Constitutional Amendment Process (1997) 8 *Constitutional Political Economy* 195; Anthony McGann, *The Tyranny of the Super-Majority: How Majority Rule protects Minorities* 10 Center for the Study of Democracy, Irvine <http://escholarship.org/uc/item/18b448r6>; McGinnis/Rappaport, 'Majority and Supermajority Rules: Three Views of the Capitol' (2007) 85 Texas Law Review 1115; Masing, 'Zwischen Kontinuität und Diskontinuität: Die Verfassungsänderung' in Wahl (ed) *Verfassungsänderung, Verfassungswandel, Verfassungsinterpretation* (2008) 131, 134; for the preservationist function discharged by select institutions *see* Bruce Ackerman, Lost Opportunity?, (1990) 10 *Tel Aviv U. Stud. L* 53, 58.

[40] *Cf* Christoph Bezemek, 'Materielle Perspektiven eines formellen Verfassungsverständnisses' in Holoubek et al (eds), *Die Zukunft der Verfassung – Verfassung der Zukunft* (2010) 437, 443-4.

[41] The possible disruption between *constitutional* laws as norms usually considered as fundamental for a community in a substantive perception and the lack of such an attribution per se in the formal conception may be exemplified quite drastically by § 10 para 2 Austrian non-scheduled services act (*Federal Gazette* 125/1987) which contained provisions for the granting of taxi-cab licenses on a *constitutional* level.

they may provide the degrading treatment of individuals with the blessing of higher lawmaking or even help the political elites in charge not to be prosecuted for crimes we do not even wish to think about; all this may be regarded as *constitutional* law whether or not to be considered as *constitutive* laws – all this enjoys the same degree of formally increased legal stability.

F. Different tiers – different weight?

The structure of the amendment provisions that serve as gatekeepers to the *constitutional* sphere, of course, differs largely. Some ask for exceptionally high requirements to be met, while others are being content with prerequisites of rather low-threshold character. Some legal systems may know only a single way of amending *constitutional* laws while others follow a tiered approach of different requirements to be met also within the *constitutional* level. The latter provide for different degrees of normative volatility approximating relative normative static within the *constitutional* sphere. This consequently entails different tiers of *constitutional* provisions causing the phenomenon that also duly enacted *constitutional* law may turn out to be un*constitutional* in case it does not comply with other *constitutional* provisions asking for additional requirements to be met in comparison with first-tier *constitutional* legislation to be lawfully altered.[42]

G. Pick and Choose

Even though many of these problems have to be reserved for deeper assessment it will be useful to keep these remarks in mind before turning to some examples of how *constitutional* amendment provisions are designed in various legal systems. It has to be noted that the examples below were chosen solely with regard to the revision mechanisms they provide for and select techniques they make use of but not with any regard to matters of substance.

In addition to that I want to emphasize that the examples below, of course, only serve to give an idea about the structural differences between different mechanisms for *constitutional* amendment. For the purpose of this essay it will not be necessary to cite any more examples, which should, of course, be part of a larger discussion of the topic. However, intellectual honestly demands to admit that also the rather superficial discussion of the examples used below is largely determined by the author's limited knowledge of the various legal systems. Thus in particular the Austrian or the US legal system will be covered

---

42 *See* for a discussion of this phenomenon Ackerman, above n 34, 15; for the continental European perspective *see*, for example, Peter Pernthaler, *Der Verfassungskern* (1998) 46, 80-1. For the Austrian Constitutional Court's case law *see* VfSlg (Collection of the Austrian Constitutional Court's Case Law) 16.327

quite broadly, whereas China, Honduras, and others will only be mentioned briefly. Due to the formal character of the model I would like to describe this should not affect the argument presented: Of course doctrinal questions (as the few discussed in this essay show) will arise against the thoughts presented below; they will, however, not determine the model's validity.

H. Form and Substance

Given that many 'rigid' constitutions not only know one single way of *constitutional* amendment but often follow a tiered approach, asking for additional requirements to be met compared to the regular form of *constitutional* amendment I want to distinguish two different techniques of such additional formal stabilization:

- A purely formal technique, focused only on procedural and institutional prerequisites – form-related stabilization
- A technique combining formal and substantive aspects by imposing additional procedural and institutional requirements if a proposed amendment is regarded to affect specific elements of the constitution – substance-related stabilization

I. A Matter of Degree

Both of these approaches anew allow for immanent gradations; thereby creating a structure within the level of *constitutional* law itself moving successively from comparatively dynamic to comparatively static *constitutional* law. These immanent graduations may be classified, essentially,[43] in three different kinds:

- Amendment
- Entrenchment
- Eternity

3) Amendment

When speaking about 'amendments' in the context of this essay I intend to use this term in a quite narrow sense. As amendment I understand the basic form of *constitutional* revision a legal system provides. Based on this understanding, amendments feature the specific characteristic that they are, when compared to

[43] Each of these classifications may anew be subdivided; most importantly a distinction can be made between implicit and explicit modes of *constitutional* revision. I will only touch on these further subdivisions for the purposes of this essay parenthetically as it will add another level of complexity to the basic model which is not necessary to explain exhaustively in order to make the main argument.

the superior modes of *constitutional* alteration, to be defined as form-related only. This is due to the fact that these mechanisms common to all 'rigid' constitutions serve as essential differentiator to the merely substantive conceptions of *constitutive* laws, concerned with creating the sphere of *constitutional* law in the first place.[44]

4) Entrenchment

The term 'entrenchment' on the other hand refers to provisions stating additional prerequisites that have to be met for the alteration of *constitutional* laws compared to the basic conception of *constitutional* amendment.

5) Eternity

'Eternity' finally, or perhaps even better: 'eternization' wants to describe provisions that go beyond entrenchment by divesting (certain parts of) the constitution of any form of revision.

Unlike amendments, entrenchment and eternization occur both on a form-related and on a substance-related level.

J. Amendment

6) Scope

To perceive amendments as basic technique of *constitutional* alteration a legal system provides, is a relational approach, comparing several mechanisms within specific legal systems; thus if a legal system should provide solely one mechanism of *constitutional* revision this would qualify as well for the purpose at hand as an amendment provision in a legal system distinguishing several kinds of differently tiered procedures of *constitutional* revision.

7) Methodical Remarks

This may seem to be a sledge-hammer-method, disregarding not only the historical and social background against which the various legal systems referred to would have to be assessed in an adequate manner but also the vast difference of the prerequisites to be met for *constitutional* amendment. However: As true as these allegations may prove to be – on a structural level they lack importance. Structurally a low threshold-character amendment provision,

[44] One may regard of course all amendment procedures as all substance-related, which is just a matter of viewpoint; a viewpoint, however, that does not prove to be very practical.

asking for any random additional requirement to be met compared to regular legislation is equivalent to an amendment provision asking for a unanimous vote in both houses of a bi-cameral system.

Still, this is not to say that the relative rigidity of amendment requirements does not matter when it comes to the question to which extent positive stabilization is permissible. Therefore a larger variety of specific examples shall be presented below in order to show that just as in life there are easy and hard cases it is the same with regard to constitutions. There are some truly amenable for amendment and there are some which are not.

a) AUSTRIA

Article 44 para 1 of the Austrian Constitution may serve as an example for the first instance:

> 'Verfassungsgesetze oder in einfachen Gesetzen enthaltene Verfassungsbestimmungen können vom Nationalrat nur in Anwesenheit von mindestens der Hälfte der Mitglieder und mit einer Mehrheit von zwei Dritteln der abgegebenen Stimmen beschlossen werden; sie sind als solche ("Verfassungsgesetz", "Verfassungsbestimmung") ausdrücklich zu bezeichnen.'[45]

These amendment requirements are rather low-threshold by their very nature.[46] The dynamic inherent to the amendment procedure of Austrian *constitutional* law evolves in particular against the backdrop of the Austrian 'Realverfassung' which largely is based on the historical bi-partisan division of the country and the mode of consensus among the conservative and the social-democratic party that culminated in longish periods when Austria was governed by a grand coalition equipped with the majorities necessary to amend the constitution anytime according to their will resulting in more than one hundred amendments to the main *constitutional* document and countless other *constitutional*

[45] 'Constitutional laws or constitutional provisions contained in simple laws can be passed by the National Council only in the presence of at least half the members and by a two thirds majority of the votes cast; they shall be explicitly specified as such ('constitutional law', 'constitutional provision').' Additionally according to Article 42 para 2 B-VG the consent of the Federal Council (Bundesrat) is required.

[46] *See*, for example, Eberhard/Lachmayer, 'Constitutional Reform 2008 in Austria' (2008) Vienna Journal on International Constitutional Law 112 <icl-journal.com>.

provisions.[47] The fragmentation caused by this practice has led to the metaphor of the Austrian Constitution as a *ruin*.[48]
Back in the time of the grand-coalition the only difference between a statutory act and a *constitutional* provision was to be found in whether or not the norm has been explicitly specified to be *constitutional* provision.[49] Bearing this in mind the safeguard-function of formal stabilization of *constitutional* law was, of course, gradually annulled as the difference between a solely substantive conception of *constitutive* laws and a formal conception of *constitutional* law was obliterated.[50]

b) CHINA

Assessing the relevant amendment provisions, without including specific political constellations abetting normative dynamic, we may add, however, that the Austrian Constitution technically states the same prerequisites for amendment as, for example, Article 64 of the Chinese constitution:

> 'Amendments to the Constitution are to be proposed by the Standing Committee of the National People's Congress or by more than one-fifth of the deputies to the National People's Congress and adopted by a vote of more than two-thirds of all the deputies to the Congress'

c) GERMANY

The requirements stated in Article 79 para 2 of the German Basic Law are quite similar to those described above for an amendment of the Austrian Constitution even though the consent requirement in the Federal Council is elevated up to two thirds:[51]

---

[47] A partial revision of the Austrian Constitution in 2008 deprived overall more than one thousand provisions of their status as constitution law.

[48] *See* Hans Klecatsky, 'Bundes-Verfassungsgesetz und Bundesverfassungsrecht' in Schambeck (ed), *Das österreichische Bundes-Verfassungsgesetz und seine Entwicklung* (1980) 83 and the critical account of Ewals Wiederin, 'Über Ruinen und Verfassungen' (2003) *juridikum* 192.

[49] For the problems connected with such broad parliamentary majorities in the Austrian system *see,* Alfred Kobzina, 'Die Flucht aus dem Verfassungsstaat' in *Festschrift Schambeck* (1994) 259 and Karl Korinek, *Verfassungsbewusstsein in Österreich* (1980).

[50] For the gradual invalidation of the basic amendment procedure in tiered systems of *constitutional* alteration below IV.A.

[51] Overall the German constitution had to experience less battery than its Austrian counterpart lacking overlong periods of grand coalitions governing the country and in absence of means to create *constitutional* law outside of the main *constitutional* document itself ('Incorporation'-Clause).

'Ein solches Gesetz bedarf der Zustimmung von zwei Dritteln der Mitglieder des Bundestages und zwei Dritteln der Stimmen des Bundesrates'[52]

d) LIECHTENSTEIN

Article 112 of the Basic Law of Liechtenstein, on the other hand, states comparatively altered prerequisites for *constitutional* amendment by stating:

> ‚Abänderungen oder allgemein verbindliche Erläuterungen dieses Grundgesetzes können sowohl von der Regierung als auch vom Landtage oder im Wege der Initiative (Art. 64) beantragt werden. Sie erfordern auf Seite des Landtages Stimmeneinhelligkeit seiner anwesenden Mitglieder oder eine auf zwei nacheinander folgenden Landtagssitzungen sich aussprechende Stimmenmehrheit von drei Vierteln derselben [...] und jedenfalls die nachfolgende Zustimmung des Landesfürsten'[53]

e) UNITED STATES

Still also the latter provision falls short of requiring high standards when compared to the regime as stated in Article V of the US constitution:[54]

---

[52] 'Any such law shall be carried by two thirds of the Members of the Bundestag and two thirds of the votes of the Bundesrat.'

[53] 'Any amendments to or universally binding interpretations of this fundamental law may be proposed either by the Government or by the Diet or through the initiative procedure (Art. 64). These shall require the approval of the Diet, either by the unanimous vote of the members present or by a majority of three-quarters of the members present [...] and in any event the subsequent assent of the Prince Regnant.'

[54] Even though not in the center of the (formal) argument presented here, it shall not be remain mentioned, however, that these demanding standards set by Art V are subject to criticism – *see*, for example, Levinson, above 38, 159-162. For an alternative approach to the amendment of the US Constitution *see* Akhil Amar, 'Philadelphia Revisited: Amending the Constitution Outside Article V' (1988) 55 *University of Chicago Law Review* 1043. For Ackerman's approach to alternative Higher Lawmaking and the tests that have to be met in this conception *see* above n 34, 290-4; *We the People: Transformations* (1998) 15-8; 'Revolution on an Human Scale' (1998-1999) 108 *Yale Law Journal* 2279, 2340-43; '2006 Oliver Wendell Holmes Lectures – The Living Constitution' (2006-2007) 120 *Harvard Law Review* 1737, 1804. For a discussion of both accounts *see* Torke, 'Extratextual Constitutional Change', 229. For one of the more recent reform proposals *see* Michael Rappaport, 'Reforming Article V: The Problems Created by the National Convention Amendment Method and how to fix them' (2010) 96 Virginia Law Review 1509.

> 'The Congress, whenever two thirds of both Houses shall deem it necessary, shall propose Amendments to this Constitution, or, on the Application of the Legislatures of two thirds of the several States, shall call a Convention for proposing Amendments, which, in either Case, shall be valid to all Intents and Purposes, as part of this Constitution, when ratified by the Legislatures of three fourths of the several States, or by Conventions in three fourths thereof, as the one or the other Mode of Ratification may be proposed by the Congress'

f) INSTRUMENT OF GOVERNMENT

Art V of the US Constitution may with regard to its rigidity may perhaps only be challenged by Article XIII of the Articles of the Confederation,[55] and, much earlier (and even more intensely), by Article VI of Cromwell's 'Instrument of Government' of 1653 stating – guided by the perception of the constitution as a treaty,[56] that could only be entered and thus only altered or dissolved unanimously[57]

> '[t]hat the laws shall not be altered, suspended, abrogated, or repealed, nor any new law made, nor any tax, charge, or imposition laid upon the people, but by common consent in Parliament [...]'

K. Entrenchment

8) Form-related Entrenchment

Entrenchment clauses typically refer to certain substantive aspects within the *constitutional* system, as civil rights, or the federal structure of the state, to give just a few examples. Some constitutions, however, also apply entrenchment mechanisms on a merely form-related level; asking for additional requirements to be met upon request *ad hoc* without specifying its object in advance.

a) LIECHTENSTEIN

In Liechtenstein, for example, according to Article 66 upon the request of the Diet (Landtag), the eligible voters or the municipalities a referendum to be held as

> '[j]edes vom Landtag beschlossene, von ihm nicht als dringlich erklärte Gesetz […], unterliegt der Volksabstimmung, wenn der Landtag eine

[55] *See* for the provision's relative rigidity, for example, Bruce Ackerman, 'Storr Lectures: Discovering the Constitution', (1984) 93 *Yale Law Journal* 1013, 1017 note 6.
[56] *See* below V.D.2.
[57] Jellinek, above n 18 511-2; also *see* Dicey, above n 10, 419.

> solche beschliesst oder wenn innerhalb von 30 Tagen nach amtlicher Verlautbarung des Landtagsbeschlusses wenigstens 1000 wahlberechtigte Landesbürger oder wenigstens drei Gemeinden [...] ein darauf gerichtetes Begehren stellen.'[58]

b) **ALBANIA**

Article 177 para 4 of the Albanian Constitution refers the question whether a referendum has to be held over a draft for *constitutional* amendment to a rather high quorum among the delegates to the assembly which

> 'may decide, with two-thirds of all its members that the draft constitutional amendments are to be voted in a referendum. The draft law for the revision of the Constitution enters into force after ratification by referendum, which takes place not later than 60 days after its approval in the Assembly'

while granting strong minority rights in article 177 para 5 in case the draft for a *constitutional* amendment has been approved in the assembly:

> 'The approved constitutional amendment has to be put to a referendum when this is required by one-fifth of the members of the Assembly'

c) **AUSTRIA**

In Austria according to Article 44 para 3 of the constitution a referendum either has to be held upon request of a third of the members of the National Council or the Federal Council or in case of a 'total revision' of the constitution:

> 'Jede Gesamtänderung der Bundesverfassung, eine Teiländerung aber nur, wenn dies von einem Drittel der Mitglieder des Nationalrates oder des Bundesrates verlangt wird, ist nach Beendigung des Verfahrens gemäß Art. 42 [consent of the Federal Council], jedoch vor der Beurkundung durch den Bundespräsidenten, einer Abstimmung des gesamten Bundesvolkes zu unterziehen.'[59]

---

58 'Every law passed by the Diet which it does not declare to be urgent [...] shall be submitted to a referendum if the Diet so decides or if not less than 1,000 citizens with the right to vote or not less than three communes submit a petition to that effect [...].'

59 'Any total revision of the Federal Constitution shall upon conclusion of the procedure pursuant to Art. 42 above but before its authentication by the Federal President be submitted

9) Substance-related Entrenchment

d) IMPLICIT SUBSTANCE-RELATED ENTRENCHMENT

The substance-related perception of the Austrian constitution's 'total-revision'-clause, mentioned before, is understood as grave alteration of the basic principles the legal system rests upon.[60] These basic principles

- Democracy
- Republicanism
- Federalism
- Rule of Law
- Separation of Powers
- Liberty

provide an additional limitation on what may be enacted by meeting solely the requirements stated for 'ordinary' *constitutional* amendments as described above. They are not explicitly mentioned in the Austrian Constitution but have to be induced from the corpus of *constitutional* law.[61]

Such an inductive approach imposes on the interpreter to deal with rather loosely definable principles. Implicit substance-related entrenchment thus raises the same methodical problems as purely substance based perceptions of *constitutional* laws;[62] asking for an induction of *constitutive* elements from a homogenous body of *constitutional* law,[63] thereby granting immense powers to the judiciary in legal systems allowing for *constitutional* adjudication.[64]

e) EXPLICIT SUBSTANCE-RELATED ENTRENCHMENT

Unlike the Austrian constitution most constitutions using means of substance-related entrenchment do not rely on a method of inductive identification of the core aspects asking for additional procedural requirements to be met but rather explicitly define the elements in question.

---

to a referendum by the entire nation, whereas any partial revision requires this only if one third of the members of the National Council or the Federal Council so demands.'

60 Theo Öhlinger, *Verfassungsrecht* (8th ed 2009) para 64.

61 *See* Andreas Janko, *Gesamtänderung der Bundesverfassung* (2004) 82.

62 Above II.

63 *See* Bezemek, above n 40, 452.

64 A power even greater, of course, with regard to eternized *constitutional* Elements – *see* Thomas Würtenberger, 'Verfassungsänderung und Verfassungswandel' in Wahl (ed) *Verfassungsänderung, Verfassungswandel, Verfassungsinterpretation* (2008) 49, 57; for the implicit entrenchment mechanism of the Indian Constitution according to the Supreme court's case law *see* His Holiness Kesavananda Bharati v The State of Kerala and Others, AIR 1973 SC 146.

i. Liechtenstein

Again Liechtenstein for example states a separate procedure in case the monarchical structure of the state shall be abolished in Article 113 of the Basic Law that has to be initiated by the voters and after a positive referendum orders the Diet to draft a republican constitution that is subject to another referendum while the Monarch is being granted the opportunity to draft a new constitution himself to be voted on at this referendum:

> ‚Wenigstens 1500 Landesbürgern steht das Recht zu, eine Initiative auf Abschaffung der Monarchie einzubringen. Im Falle der Annahme der Initiative durch das Volk hat der Landtag eine neue Verfassung auf republikanischer Grundlage auszuarbeiten und diese frühestens nach einem Jahr und spätestens nach zwei Jahren einer Volksabstimmung zu unterziehen. Dem Landesfürsten steht das Recht zu, für die gleiche Volksabstimmung eine neue Verfassung vorzulegen.'[65]

Entrenching only a single aspect of the constitution on a substance-related level however is comparatively rare. Mostly constitutions that operate with these mechanisms safeguard a multitude of core-principles by using this technique:

ii. Bangladesh

Article 142 para 1A of the Constitution of Bangladesh may serve as an example for this approach entrenching the fundamental principles underlying the constitution[66] that are – unlike demonstrated above with the help of Article 44 para 3 of the Austrian constitution – explicitly referred to as well (including the provisions dealing with the status of the president and the ministers and the entrenchment clause itself):

---

[65] 'Not less than 1,500 citizens as a minimum requirement have the right to introduce an initiative to abolish the Monarchy. In the event of this proposal being accepeted by the People, the Diet shall draw up a new, republican Constitution and submit it to a referendum after one year at the earliest and two years at the latest. The Prince Regnant has the right to submit a new Constitution for the same referendum.'

[66] *See* Article 8 para 1 of the Constitution of Bangladesh: 'The principles of absolute trust and faith in the Almighty Allah, nationalism, democracy and socialism meaning economic and social justice, together with the principles derived from them as set out in this Part, shall constitute the fundamental principles of state policy.'

> 'when a Bill [is] passed [...] which provides for the amendment of the Preamble or any provisions of articles 8, 48 [or] 56 or this article, is presented to the President for assent, the President, shall within the period of seven days, after the Bill is presented to him, cause to be referred to a referendum the question whether the Bill should or should not be assented to.'

iii. Iraq

The path chosen in Article 122 para 2 of the Iraqi constitution is comparable even though it sets standards that are more demanding than the requirements stated by its Bangladeshi counterpart:

> 'The fundamental principles mentioned in Section One and the rights and liberties mentioned in Section Two of the Constitution may not be amended except after two successive electoral terms, with the approval of two-thirds of the Council of Representatives members, and the approval of the people in a general referendum and the ratification of the President of the Republic within seven days.'

iv. Austria

Also the Austrian constitution, however, is not being exclusively content with the inductive approach and does contain instances of *explicit* substance-related entrenchment safeguarding the states' powers by stating in Article 44 para 2

> ‚Verfassungsgesetze oder in einfachen Gesetzen enthaltene Verfassungsbestimmungen, durch die die Zuständigkeit der Länder in Gesetzgebung oder Vollziehung eingeschränkt wird, bedürfen überdies der in Anwesenheit von mindestens der Hälfte der Mitglieder und mit einer Mehrheit von zwei Dritteln der abgegebenen Stimmen zu erteilenden Zustimmung des Bundesrates.' [67]

and stating in Article 34 para 4 additional requirements for the enactment of a *constitutional* provision affecting the Federal Council's composition:

---

[67] 'Constitutional laws or constitutional provisions contained in simple laws restricting the competence of the Laender in legislation or execution require furthermore the approval of the Federal Council which must be imparted in the presence of at least half the members and by a two thirds majority of the votes cast'.

> 'Die Bestimmungen der Art 34 und 35 können nur abgeändert werden, wenn im Bundesrat - abgesehen von der für seine Beschlussfassung überhaupt erforderlichen Stimmenmehrheit - die Mehrheit der Vertreter von wenigstens vier Ländern die Änderung angenommen hat.'[68]

Article 44 para 2 of the Austrian Constitution again, shares similarities to Article 122 para 4 of the Iraqi Constitution even though with regard to the Republic of Iraq there are higher requirements to be met in case the powers of the regions are affected.

v. Iraq

> 'Articles of the constitution may not be amended if such amendment takes away from the powers of the regions that are not within the exclusive powers of the federal authorities except by the consent of the legislative authority of the concerned region and the approval of the majority of its citizens in a general referendum.'

vi. United States

Article 34 para 4 of the Austrian Constitution, however, clearly shows similarities to the explicit substance-related provision in the US Constitution, stating at the end of Article V

> 'that no State, without its Consent, shall be deprived of its equal Suffrage in the Senate.'

which of course sets standards that go far beyond the Austrian constitution's four-states rule as described above;[69] causing Bryce to call it in this respect 'virtually, if not technically, unchangeable'.[70]

---

68 'Article 34 and 35 can only be altered if – in addition to the majority required for constitutional amendment – a majority of the representatives of at least four of the Laender in the Federal Council has consented to the amendment'.

69 For the history of this part of the provision *see*, for example, Sanford Levinson, ''Veneration'' and Constitutional Change: James Madison Confronts the Possibility of Constitutional Amendment' (1990) 21 *Tex. Techh. L. Rev.* 2443 246-7.

70 Bryce, above n 14, 209.

L. Eternity

Apart from such 'virtually unchangeable constitutional' provisions we may encounter constitutions which actually are defined as – at least partially – unalterable: the phenomenon of *eternization*.

10) Form-related Eternity

Applying the model of form- and substance-related stabilization as introduced above the conclusion may be obvious that the only opportunity of creating purely form-related eternization[71] may be to declare the constitution unalterable as a whole.[72]

Examples for unalterable constitutions are rare, of course. Complete petrifaction has been considered in France 1789, when the question of whether or not a constitution should be an amendable document or rather a secluded system was discussed controversially; however, this approach has not been adapted eventually.[73] Obviously this approach was carried into effect by the *Charte constitutionnelle française* of 1814 granted by Louis XVIII which did not provide for the case of amendment.[74] Evidently this approach was unsuccessful. Bryce commented on this with the words: 'Nothing human is immortal; and constitutionmakers do well to remember that the less they presume on the long life of their work the longer it is likely to live'.[75]

11) Substance-related Eternity

It seems though that modern *constitutionmakers* did not heed Bryce's advice. Or at least that they did not heed his advice fully. An immense number of modern Constitutions avail themselves of eternity clauses explicitly specifying unalterable aspects.

f) IMPLICIT SUBSTANCE-RELATED ETERNITY

The first eternity clause in the sense it is understood nowadays is found in Article 112 of the Norwegian Constitution of 1814.

i. Norway

---

[71] However intellectual honesty demands to state that the classification of Constitutions which are *a priori* unalterable as form-related may eventually turn out to be a question of viewpoint. Thought out one may as well reach the result that eternization of a whole constitution is nothing but the substance-related stabilization referring not only to single aspects but to *each* aspect of the constitution.

[72] *See* for a discussion of this phenomenon Kelsen, above n 30, 253-4.

[73] *See* Carl Schmitt, Verfassungslehre (9th ed Reprint 2003) 10.

[74] *Cf* Jellinek, above n 18, 527.

[75] Bryce, above n 14, 208.

'[An] amendment must never, however, contradict the principles embodied in this Constitution, but solely relate to modifications of particular provisions which do not alter the spirit of the Constitution, and such amendment requires that two thirds of the Storting agree thereto.'

g) EXPLICIT SUBSTANCE-RELATED ETERNITY

ii. France 3rd Republic

The French *constitutional* laws of 1875 establishing the Third Republic as amended by the *constitutional* law of August 14th 1884 explicitly prohibited a change into a form of *constitutional* monarchy by stating:

'La forme républicaine du gouvernement ne peut faire l'objet d'une proposition de revision'

iii. Tonga

Article 79 of the constitution of Tonga, also dating back to 1875, again, quite on the opposite, preserved (among other central concepts) the monarchical structure of the state by stating

'amendments shall not affect the law of liberty the succession to the Throne and the titles and hereditary estates of the nobles'

iv. Germany

The most prominent example of such an eternity clause is, of course, to be found in Article 79 paragraph 3 of the German Basic Law stating:

‚Eine Änderung dieses Grundgesetzes, durch welche die Gliederung des Bundes in Länder, die grundsätzliche Mitwirkung der Länder bei der Gesetzgebung oder die in den Artikeln 1 und 20 niedergelegten Grundsätze berührt werden, ist unzulässig'[76]

v. Italy

[76] 'Amendments to this Basic Law affecting the division of the Federation into *Laender*, their participation on principle in the legislative process, or the principles laid down in Articles 1 and 20 shall be inadmissible.'

Also, Article 139 of the Italian Constitution contains an eternity-clause even though its textual scope is limited in comparison with its German counterpart:

> 'La forma repubblicana non può essere oggetto di revisione costituzionale'

vi. *Democratic Republic of the Congo*

Eternity-Clauses like those mentioned above, however, are not elements predominantly peculiar to Western European constitutions. Quite the contrary we find impressive examples for most elegantly elaborated versions of *constitutional* Eternity-clauses in *constitutional* provisions like Article 220 of the Constitution of the Democratic Republic of the Congo

> 'La forme républicaine de l'État, le principe du suffrage universel, la forme représentative du Gouvernement, le nombre et la durée des mandats du Président de la République, l'indépendance du Pouvoir judiciaire, le pluralisme politique et syndical, ne peuvent faire l'objet d'aucune révision constitutionnelle'

vii. *Honduras*

We find similar approaches in Article 374 of the constitution of Honduras,

> 'No podrán reformarse, en ningún caso, el artículo anterior [constitutional amendment provision], el presente artículo, los artículos constitucionales que se refieren a la forma de gobierno, al territorio nacional, al período presidencial, a la prohibición para ser nuevamente Presidente de la República, el ciudadano que lo haya desempeñado bajo cualquier título y el referente a quienes no pueden ser Presidentes de la República por el período subsiguiente'

or in Article 225 of the constitution of Chad

viii. *Chad*

> 'No procedure of revision may be started or pursued if it interferes with:
> – the integrity of the territory, independence or national unity;
> – the republican form of the state, the principle of the division of powers and secularity;

- the freedoms and fundamental rights of the citizen;
- political pluralism.'

ix. Afghanistan

In Article 149 of the Islamic Republic of Afghanistan's Constitution; a clause that provides an interesting example not only because of the safeguard-provision with respect to Islam but in particular because of its 'Favorability-Clause' with regard to the fundamental rights granted by the constitution's second chapter

> 'The principles of adherence to the tenets of the Holy religion of Islam as well as Islamic Republicanism shall not be amended. Amending fundamental rights of the people shall be permitted only to improve them.'

x. Democratic Republic of the Congo

which again may be compared to the quite similar Article 220 of the Democratic Republic of the Congo safeguarding fundamental rights:

> 'Est formellement interdite toute révision constitutionnelle ayant pour objet ou pour effet de réduire les droits et libertés de la personne, ou de réduire les prérogatives des provinces et des entités territoriales décentralisées.'

Of course many more examples could be added to those cited above. One could point at the eternization of the amnesty granted to those involved in various coups d'état by Article 141 of the Constitution of Niger's 5th Republic or to the positive presupposition of the Holy Qur'an as the Constitution's foundation in Article 7 of the Basic Law of the Kingdom of Saudi Arabia. However, the various techniques have been demonstrated sufficiently.

M. Lessons

12) Dynamic – Static

At the beginning of this essay I admitted its task would rather be to ask questions than to provide answers. However, looking back at what has been said, there are also some lessons to be learned; lessons, of course, that may raise another plurality of questions.

The most obvious conclusion is that when assessed from the positive perspective 'flexible' systems, like the UK constitution, are at the same time (to translate it to the terms used in this essay) inherently 'dynamic', whereas 'rigid' constitutions overall reduce this dynamic, shifting the legal system towards a 'static' design.[77]

However, it would not have taken dozens of pages to reach this result. Perhaps of greater interest is the observation that the *constitutional* sphere created by the means of formal stabilization is not a monolithic block. The distinction between ordinary legislation and *constitutional* law turns out not to be a line of demarcation but a border region where more than one checkpoint has to be passed: Rather the term *constitutional* laws refers to different layers that grant a greater extent of dynamic to some *constitutional* provisions while specifically denying it to others. Based on the model introduced above also within the *constitutional* sphere of a legal system elements of rather dynamic or rather static character can be distinguished: Already when analyzing purely form-related techniques of stabilization we often witness a tiered system: additional requirements may have to be met compared to those stated in the constitution's basic amendment provision (form-related Entrenchment) or the constitution as such may be unalterable as a whole (form-related Eternization) – resulting in a formally static constitution.[78]

A multitude of formal *constitutional* systems, however, partially turn to a substantive conception,[79] positively defining certain aspects that are considered fundamental and stating elevated prerequisites for their alteration (substance-related Entrenchment) or prohibit their alteration overall (substance-related Eternization).[80]

The phenomenon analyzed may thus be described as a movement from normative dynamic towards normative static due to the introduction of the (fragmented) sphere of *constitutional* laws: The formal distinction between ordinary legislation and *constitutional* law entails the stabilization of the latter, a stabilization that keeps progressing positively up to the point of the constitution's (partial) eternization – creating normative static; a

[77] Above III.
[78] Above III.G.2.
[79] Above III.I.2.
[80] Above III.J.2.

'Foundationalist' system.[81] I hope the examples I referred to, gave a basic idea of how the various techniques of positive stabilization are actually applied.

13) Is - Ought

Compared to legal systems guided by a substantive perception of *constitutive* laws, legal systems introducing *constitutional* laws rather clearly state which laws are to be considered of particular gravity; which is, as we have seen, a rather arbitrary choice: Anything – non-scheduled services, prohibition, slavery as well as civil rights – may have its share of *constitutional* authority as long as specified requirements are met. The model sketched above provides us with a tool for the analysis of a given legal system with regard to its comparatively dynamic and static components which allows us to assess legal systems according to the questions which key features they are trying to safeguard and to what extent they do so, within a certain legal system as well as in comparison with other legal systems. It does not, however, provide us with any criteria to answer the question what ought (or ought not) to be positively stabilized.

IV. *The pre-positive perspective*

N. The Earth and the Living Generation

But may the question, which normative content ought or ought not to be *constitutionally* protected, entrenched, or eternized legitimately answered anyway? Rousseau's answer, for example, that the more important the question discussed the higher the requirements to be met,[82] does not prove to be helpful: In a positive perspective the system offers a great extent of permeability; it is form that counts, not substance. Positively, the phenomenon of eternization has to be seen as terminal point of the vector leading from normative dynamic to normative static. Still, this leaves many questions unanswered:

– May eternity clauses be created within systems yet unfamiliar with this instrument?

– May revision clauses be lawfully amended (in case they do not state otherwise)?

– ...

O. Grundnorm vs Principle-Guided Norm Presupposition

A general answer addressing these questions, whatever it may be, will not be found when approaching the question from a doctrinal perspective; it must not be phrased on a *positive*, but on a *pre*-positive level.

---

81 Ackerman, above n 34, 15.

82 Rousseau, *Du contract Social* IV Ch II.

On this *pre*-positive level, of course, many different anchor points may be distinguished. Still, I would like to focus on only two of them, assuming, without oversimplifying excessively, that both conceptions eventually do cover a quite broad range of the most significant theoretical approaches:[83] A Kelsenian 'Grundnorm' conception and a Conception based on a 'natural law' approach.

Both approaches are designed to provide a theoretical foundation for legal systems thereby granting legitimacy to (decide on the validity of) positive law. Both struggle with (different) problems I need not to address in this essay. The assumption of a 'Grundnorm'[84] as a necessary theoretical precondition of any legal system[85] proves to be particularly unsatisfactory, however, for the task at hand; not (only) with regard to the frequent objections this theory had (has) to face[86] but (also) because in Kelsen's own understanding of 'the content of the positive legal order [as] completely independent of the basic norm from which only the objective validity of the norms of the positive legal order, not the content of this order, can be derived'.[87] Grundnorm-doctrine *per se* will not provide us with criteria for the *Ought* or the *Ought Not* of formally elevated, entrenched, and eternized normative content.

Therefore one may consider to turn towards the definition of a pre-positive structure that allows for the analysis of a legal order's content presupposing a principle deriving from the idea of a social compact;[88] a compact idea as underlying,[89] for example, in the US Constitution.[90]

---

83 *Cf*, for example, Alfred Verdross, *Abendländische Rechtsphilosophie* (2nd ed 1963) 192.

84 For Kelsen's own account *see*, in particular, above n 30, 250-3 and Reine Rechtslehre (2nd ed 1960) 196-199 and, of course, 'On the Basic Norm' (1959) 47 *California Law Review* 107, 109-10.

85 *See*, for example Robert Walter, Wirksamkeit und Geltung (1961) 11 *Zeitschrift für öffentliches Recht* 531, 537.

86 Just *see* Julius Stone, 'Mystery and Mystique in the Basic Norm' (1983) 26 *Modern Law Rev* 34.

87 Hans Kelsen, Professor Stone and the Pure Theory of Law (1964-65) 17 *Stanford Law Review* 1128, 1141-2.

88 I do realize, of course, that these approaches – at least when coming from a Kelsenian perspective – do not match one another. A conception of a *Grundnorm* which is deemed to be void will not allow for any substantive attribution from the very outset, rendering the following thoughts useless.

89 I am, of course, not assuming a contract determined by a specific context out of which a genesis of normative legitimacy shall be developed as Kelsen obviously does – *see* Allgemeine Staatslehre 251.

90 *Cf* James Madison, *Federalist* No. 44 (1788) – edited by Jacob E. Cooke (1961) referring to Bills of attainder, ex post facto laws and laws impairing the obligation of contracts as 'contrary to the first principles of the social compact.'

P. Christianity as State Religion

Let us take an example provided by Bruce Ackerman to sketch the basic idea by assuming a successful campaign for partial repeal of the first amendment introducing a *constitutional* provision whereas:

> 'Christianity is established as the state religion of the American people and the public worship of other gods is hereby forbidden.'

Against the backdrop of this example Ackerman argues vividly that if he was a member of the Supreme Court in those days he would either reject a petition to declare the amendment un*constitutional* or 'resign [...] office and join in a campaign to convince the American people to change their mind.'[91] In this scenario Ackerman's Dualist Theory trumps Rights Foundationalism. This is a fair point. But will this perception of strict Dualism prove to be successful as the constitution's last frontier?

What if the amendment in question was designed in a way that would not allow any advocacy in opposition to its content or more radically: What if 'the American People' decide to introduce a *constitutional* principle abolishing freedom of speech overall? What if 'The People', by vast majority decide to introduce an eternity clause to the constitution abandoning any popular political participation, be it on the present level of normal politics, be it with regard to any future revision of the *constitutional* structure? To put it bluntly:

> Is it open to 'The People' to abolish a constitution's democratic structure, just like Mo the bartender once famously suggested?[92]

Q. Beyond Dualism (II)?

14) Dark Days

Ackerman of course sees the point even though referring to the main problem only in a footnote, summing it up by stating that '[s]uch questions are best left to the dark day they arise'[93] – an approach that may be considered to be pragmatic. However, it is an approach accepting that there is an answer to be found, be it today or Ackerman's dark day. Interestingly, once we accept this possibility we also have to accept that this answer has to be true for today as

---

91 Ackerman, above n 34, 14.

92 'Who wants to abolish democracy forever? Show of Hands!', The Simpsons, Season 19 Episode 10 – E. Pluribus Wiggum.

93 Ackerman, above n 34, 16.

well as for future days to come as it has to lead 'Beyond Dualism', beyond *a specific* legal system.

15) A participatory Grundnorm?

h) 'CONSENT OF THE GOVERNED'

One thought that may be developed derives from the popular consent *in abstracto* as precondition underlying these conceptions, forming the foundation of the *pre-constitutional pouvoir constituant originaire*[94] which consequently can be altered only by such consent. When Rousseau, for example, assumes that the collective henceforth decides to accept the majority's decision in her place,[95] this assumption is based on the fact that as a matter of principle the possibility of a change of majority and by that the individual's opportunity to participate in public decision-making is being preserved. It is this opportunity to participation that serves as pre-supposed structural principle:[96] Indeed, '[t]he Constitution presupposes a citizenry with a sound grasp of the distinctive ideals that inspire its political practice'.[97]

i) SNAPSHOTS AND STRUCTURAL PRINCIPLES

A possible argument would have to originate from the abstract (and thus, to put it in the terms used in this essay, static) idea of common consent to delegate decisions to a majority, a delegation that may again only be invalidated by such common consent *in abstracto*. To sacrifice this holistic approach for a snapshot of a momentary decision to abolish the state's democratic structure is not an option under this concept as the snapshot would only show a volition within the limits of the *pouvoir constituant institué*: If perceived in a different way an arbitrary cross-section of specific subjects would be entrusted to abolish what has not been transferred to its discretion but has rather been entrusted to be preserved for all future subjects.

Following this argument not even the consent of an entire people to establish a dictatorship would change this assessment: A principle of participation

94 For the origin of the distinction between *pouvoir constituant originaire* and *pouvoir constituant institué, see* Sieyès classical work, *Qu'est-ce que le tiers-état?*.

95 Rousseau, above n 82, I Ch V.

96 *See* for various conceptions and the idea of participation in the social compact model: Immanuel Kant, *Allgemeine Geschichte in Weltbürgerlicher Absicht* (Akademie Edition VIII) 23; Thomas Paine, *Common Sense and the Rights of Men* (Signet 2003) 6-7; Thomas Hobbes, *Leviathan* (Yale 2010) XVIII; Locke, *Second Treatise of Government* (Edition Millar 1764) § 95; Rousseau above n 82, I Ch. V; Nozick, *Anarchy, State, and Utopia* (1974) 113-120.

97 Ackerman, above n 34, 3.

underlying the *pouvoir constituant originaire*, may not be abolished by the means of momentarily democratic decision making which is nothing but the basic structure's single manifestation. A snapshot of a volition within the limits of the *pouvoir constituant institué* does not dispose of the conditions necessary for such a structural change; these are different levels – a *positive* on the one and a *pre-*positive on the other hand. Again (but in a different relation than introduced before) this snapshot may be perceived as 'Normal (*constitutional*) Politics' concerned with decisions immanent to the system but not about transcending the system's preconditions. What this approach does reflect clearly is the spirit of Article 28 of the *Declaration des droits de l'homme et du citoyen of 1793*:

> 'Un peuple a toujours le droit de revoir, de réformer et de changer sa Constitution. *Une génération ne peut assujettir à ses lois les générations futures*'[98]

But does it relate to the question of dynamic and static analysis? The answer would be in the affirmative: If it proves to be valid, the argument teaches us that beyond all possible *positively* created normative static, participation as a principle deriving from the legal system's static *precondition* of common consent has to be presupposed; a presupposition that cannot be overcome by the positive means of normative stabilization.

R. And back?

By means of this pre-positive principle of participation the apparent antagonism of normative dynamic and normative static may be dissolved: What the principle would vouch for would be nothing but to grant dynamic; ultimately then change is what remains as a legal system's unalterable foundation: the people's chance to change their mind.

Coming from this perspective the doctrinal structure elaborated above has to be reevaluated. It will take careful analysis to define the permissible range of positively abetted normative static against the backdrop of this pre-positive principle and to see whether and to what extent positive stabilization has to be considered to be legitimate options of positive stabilization. However, we may state already at this point that the amendment provision prohibiting any advocacy against the 'Christianity-Amendment' may prove to be incompatible with the theory introduced above. Not because the approach introduced is foundationalist in character but on the contrary because it is committed essentially to a dualist (or perhaps: trialist) conception; 'it is democratic first,

[98] Emphasis added by author.

rights protecting second'[99] as rights, according to this theory, derive from the structural principle of participation – committed to prevent the 'repeal of [Dualist] Democracy itself';[100] ensuring the earth would still belong 'to the living generation'.[101]

[99] Ackerman, above n 39, 62.
[100] Ackerman, above n 34, 16.
[101] Discussing the way Jefferson's approached this demand Robert McDonald, 'Thomas Jefferson and Historical Self-Construction: The Earth Belongs to the Living?' (1999) 61 *The Historian* 289.

LAW AND FLEXIBILITY
- RULE OF LAW LIMITS OF A RHETORICAL SILVER BULLET -

Lutz-Christian Wolff*

1. Introduction

It has often been argued that legal rules and their application have to be flexible in order to allow for just decisions in individual cases. Flexibility is sometimes even regarded as a distinguishing feature of the common law as such. Taking these claims as a starting point this article explores the significance of flexibility from the viewpoint of the rule of law doctrine. It demonstrates that flexibility is not rule of law-compatible. In order to uphold the rule of law it is therefore necessary to prove that there is no flexibility. *Vice versa*, if it turns out that the law offers flexibility then the rule of law doctrine has to be reconsidered.

A sharpened awareness of the use of words can sharpen the awareness of phenomena.[1] The word 'flexibility' has been and is used in many different ways and the discussion of flexibility touches upon a great variety of phenomena of very general nature. It is not within the scope of this article to contribute substantially to these debates. In particular, it cannot be the goal of this article to have the last word on the jurisprudential significance of flexibility or to discuss flexibility from the viewpoint of the empirical reality of law in action. In contrast, this article tries to draw attention to the doctrinal determination of flexibility. In particular, this article aims at emphasizing the limitations potentially imposed by the rule of law doctrine on the use of the word 'flexibility' for argumentative purposes.

Divided into three parts this article first narrows down the meaning of 'flexibility' and similar notions by exploring what this term might imply and how it has been used in practice. It goes on to analyze in its main part how flexibility fits into the framework of the rule of law doctrine, more precisely how flexibility interacts with the notion of legal certainty. The final part then summarizes the findings and draws conclusions of a more general nature.[2]

---

*Professor of Law, Faculty of Law – The Chinese University of Hong Kong.

[1] R.S. Summers, The New Analytical Jurists (1966) 41 New York University Law Review, 861-869, 862, with reference to J. L. Austin, A Plea for Excuses, (1956-57) 57 Proceedings of the Aristotelian Society 1-30, 8.

[2] This article is a result of self-reflection. Like many others I have used the term 'flexibility' without acknowledging its interaction with the rule of law doctrine, see *eg* L.-Ch. Wolff, "Statutory Retention of Title Structures?" (2009) 14 Deakin L. Rev. 1-27, 27. The criticism in

2. Delineating Flexibility

Any discussion of 'flexibility' must begin with a definition of this term. This causes some difficulties as 'flexibility' is not an established legal concept nor is there a commonly acknowledged definition or way in which 'flexibility' is used in the legal context. While it is consequently not surprising that lines of discussion that are based on or driven by the call for flexibility often appear to be somewhat unfocused, arguments mainly point in the following four different directions.

Firstly, flexibility is apparently often understood as an intrinsic feature of legal rules. For example, in the context of the discussions regarding the introduction of European conflict of laws regimes in England it has been argued that "the technique of building an element of flexibility into rules of applicable law is a notable feature of English private international law, both judge made and in statutory form".[3]

Secondly, one may regard flexibility as an attribute of the application of the law. From this perspective, it would not be the law itself that is flexible, but how the law is applied in practice.[4]

Thirdly, flexibility has been regarded as a distinguishing feature of the common law. Scarman J. has made this point in *McLoughlin v O'Brien*:[5]

> "By concentrating on principle the judges can keep the Common Law alive, flexible and consistent, and can keep the legal system clear of policy problems which neither they, nor the forensic process which it is their duty to operate, are equipped to resolve.
>
> …
>
> The real risk of Common Law is not its movement to cover new situations and new knowledge but lest it should stand still, halted by a conservative judicial approach. If that should happen … there would be a

---

the following chapters of the sometimes rather loose use of 'flexibility' is therefore first and foremost addressed to me.

3 A. Dickinson, "Third-Country Mandatory Rules in the Law Applicable to Contractual Obligations: So Long, Farewell, Auf Wiedersehen, Adieu?"(2007) 3 J. Priv. Int'l L. 53-88, 64; *cf.* in more detail *infra*, chapter 3.1.

4 *Cf.* A. Mills, "The Dimension of Public Policy in Private International Law" (2008) 4 J. Priv. Int'l L. 201-236, 336; *cf.* in more detail *infra*, chapter 3.2.

5 *McLoughlin v. O'Brien* [1983] 1 AC 410; *cf.* in more detail *infra*, chapter 3.3.

danger of the law becoming irrelevant to the consideration, and inept in its treatment, of modern social problems. Justice would be defeated. The Common Law has, however, avoided this catastrophe by the flexibility given it by generations of judges."[6]

The claim that case law is more flexible than codified rules[7] may be regarded as a variation of the argument that flexibility is one of the characteristics of the common law.[8]

Finally, flexibility has also been discussed as a potential feature of the form legal rules may take. From this viewpoint "flexible rules" have been described as rules which "grant discretion with or without standards for its exercise, or [incorporation of] vague concepts such as 'reasonableness'".[9]

The different applications of the term 'flexibility' may of course imply differences also *vis-à-vis* their respective doctrinal viability. Related issues will therefore be explored separately in the following sections.

3. Flexibility and the Law

3.1 The Flexibility of Legal Rules

3.1.1 General

As mentioned in the previous section, flexibility is often seen as an intrinsic feature of legal rules. Unfortunately, courts and commentators normally fail to elaborate further on related specifics. It appears, however, that flexible rules are meant to be rules which are open-ended thus not offering guidance as to what the law is in relation to particular issues. According to this understanding flexible rules therefore do not determine their respective application outcome.[10]

---

6 Also *cf.* C. Perelman, *Justice, Law, and Argument* (Dordrecht/Boston 1980), 39-40; J. Harris, "Understanding the English Response to the Europeanisation of Private International Law" (2008) 4 J. Priv. Int'l L. 347-395, 359.
7 Lord Wilberforce, Hansard HL col. 840 (6 December 1994).
8 *Cf.* in more detail *infra*, chapter 3.4.
9 P.S. Atiyah and R.S. Summers, *Form and Substance in Anglo-American Law* (Oxford 1987) 71-88; *cf.* in more detail *infra*, chapter 3.5.
10 Dickinson (note 3), 82.

The proposition of rule-inherent flexibility is normally accompanied by the acknowledgement of a particular "tension"[11] between flexibility on the one hand and legal certainty on the other. Andrew Dickinson has summarized this understanding when stating that "a measure of uncertainty must be accepted as a necessary consequence of the flexibility." [12] Others[13] have made reference to Lord Scarman[14] who had argued that "the search for certainty can obstruct the law's pursuit of justice, and can become the enemy of the good." Rule-inherent flexibility is therefore not seen as an inadvertent effect. In contrast, flexibility is intended and regarded as necessary to allow just decisions in individual cases.[15]

Legal rules with flexible contents must be distinguished from rules from which deviation is possible within the framework of other "superior legal commands".[16] This kind of deviation is rule-based and not open-ended[17] and does therefore not lead to the issues addressed in this article. Flexible rules must also be distinguished from rules that change as a result of the historical development of the law within its social, economic and political setting.[18] These changes take place over time and do not necessarily imply flexibility of the law at a particular moment.

3.1.2 The Problem: Legal Certainty *vs* Flexibility

The definition of rule-intrinsic flexibility in the previous section leads to two questions: Is rule-intrinsic flexibility allowable from the viewpoint of the rule of law doctrine? If the answer to this question is 'no', what does this mean for the claim that flexibility is required to achieve justice in individual cases? To

---

11 *Cf.* Sir A. Mason, "The Use and Abuse of Precedent" (1988) 4 Australian Bar Review 93-111, 95; M. Kirby, Precedent Law, Practice & Trends in Australia, <http://www.hcourt.gov.au/speeches/kirbyj/kirbyj_dec06.pdf> accessed 30 May 2010, 14; W. Morrison, A. Geary and R. Jago, *The Politics of the Common Law* (London/New York 2008) W. Morrison, A. Geary and R. Jago, *The Politics of the Common Law* (London/New York 2008) 94.

12 Dickinson (note 3) 82.

13 Morrison, Geary and Jago (note 11) 89.

14 *McLoughlin v. O'Brian* [1983] 1 AC 410, 430.

15 Dickinson (note 3) 82; also *cf.* Mason (note 11) 95; Morrison, Geary and Jago (note 11) 89; R. Pound, *An Introduction to the Philosophy of Law* (New Haven/London 1922) 71;

16 O. Ben-Shahar, "The Tentative Case Against Flexibility in Commercial Law", (1999) 66 U. Chicago Law Review, 781-820, 785 (for the discussion of the US Uniform Commercial Code allowing unwritten commercial practices to vary express contractual provisions).

17 *Cf.* Ben-Shahar, *ibid.*, 785.

18 *Cf.* Perelman, (note 6), 131, 164; R. Stammler, *Wirtschaft und Recht*, 5th ed., (Leipzig 1924), 174, had pointed out that natural law inevitably has a variable content and is not fixed once and forever, *cf* A. Fouillee *et al.*, *Modern French Legal Philosphy* (transl. by F.W. Scott and J.P. Chamberlain) (New York 1921 – reprinted Holmes Beach 1998), 106-111, 111.

answer these questions one must take a closer look at the described tension between flexibility on the one hand and legal certainty on the other.[19]

Legal certainty is a direct result of predictability.[20] Not just since the publication of Dicey's famous work[21] in 1885 legal certainty is seen as one of the main pillars of the rule of law doctrine which itself is said to embody the 'absolute supremacy or predominance of regular law'.[22] The rule of law and thus legal certainty are regarded as the basis of the common law.[23]

Legal certainty is not regarded as simply an aesthetic requirement. The benefits of legal certainty have been discussed broadly and are commonly acknowledged. Most importantly, legal certainty is the *conditio sine qua non* for the law to be applied equally to all persons in like circumstances in a non-arbitrary manner.[24] Only to the extent that the law is transparent and that the outcome of its application is predictable will everybody know which behaviour is required to achieve or avoid the consequences of the law.[25] In contrast, access to justice

---

[19] *Supra,* chapter 3.1.1.
[20] *Cf.*, however, M. A. Chibundu, Globalizing the Rule of Law: Some Thoughts At and on the Periphery, (1999) 7 Indiana Journal of Global Legal Studies, 79 – 116 (88-89).
[21] *Cf.* A.V. Dicey, *Introduction to the Study of the Law of the Constitution* (10th edn St. Martin's Press, New York 1959) 183-414.
[22] *Ibid.* 202; *cf.* Morrison, Geary and Jago (note 11) 14; T. Bingham, Rt. Hon. Lord, House of Lords, "The Sixth Sir David Williams Lecture: The Rule of Law" [2006] <http://www.cpl.law.com.ac.uk/Media/THE%20RULE%20)F%20LAW%202006.pdf > accessed 30 May 2010, para. 10; *Mason* (note 11) 93; R. Stein, "Rule of Law: What Does it Mean?" (2009) 18 Minn.J.Int'l L. 293-303, 302; T. J. Zywicki, "The Rule of Law, Freedom, And Prosperity" (2003) 10 Sup. Ct. Econ. Rev. 1- 26,12-13, 15; B. Z. Tamanaha, "A Concise Guide to the Rule of Law" in G. Palombella and N. Walker (eds), *Relocating the Rule of Law* (Oxford/Portland 2009) 3-15, 3; *cf.* Neil MacCormick, Rhetoric and the Rule of Law, in David Dyzenhaus, Recrafting the Rule of Law: The Limits of Legal Order (Oxford/Portland: Hart Publishing, 1999), 163-177 (163): "Values like legal certainty and legal security are much lauded in the context of praising the rule of law.".
[23] Morrison, Geary and Jago (note 11) 72: "... Common Law systems ... specify that predictability and recognisability of law arc fcatures of their system."; also *cf.* Harris, (note 6) 360; N. MacCormick, *Rhetoric and the Rule of Law* (Oxford: Oxford University Press, 2005), 2; Christopher A. Whytock, "Myth or Mess? International Choice of Law in Action", (2009) 84 New York University Law Review, 719-790 (735-736), discussing negative impacts of the lack of predictability on global governance, global economic welfare and the transnational rule of law.
[24] Lord Bingham (note 22) para. 10; Stein (note 229) 302; Tamanaha 2009 (note 22) 10-11.
[25] Mason (note 11) 93: "In order that the citizen may order his affairs and make decisions, the courts must apply uniformly rules and principles that are ascertainable in advance."; F. Schauer, "Precedent" (1986-1987) 39 Stanford L. Rev. 571-605, 597; MacCormick 2005 (note 22) 3, 12, 16; Tamanaha 2009 (note 22) 6; Atiyah and Summers (note 9), 73; E. Paunio, "Beyond Predictability – Reflections on Legal Certainty and the Discourse Theory of Law in the EU Legal Order", (2009) 10 German Law Journal (No. 11), 1469-1493 (1469).

would be compromised if the law was not transparent and the outcome of the application of the law was not predictable. Moreover, an arbitrary application of the law can only be prevented to the extent that rules and their application are predictable, *ie* that the law is certain.[26] It has been said that legal certainty consequently avoids disputes, decreases expenses and increases profits.[27]

In light of these rule of law features rule-inherent elements of flexibility do not appear to be permissible. As explained, flexible rules are open-ended in that they do not mandate a particular application outcome. Predictability is therefore unachievable by flexible rules. In other words, rule-inherent flexibility and legal certainty seem to be incompatible. Flexible rules should consequently not have a place in any rule of law-based system. Flexible rules may even be unconstitutional in countries e.g. like England where the constitution itself is based on the rule of law.[28] Accordingly, the claim that the law provides for flexible rules and is at the same time rule of law-based may have to be regarded as a *contradictio in adjecto*.[29]

Conclusions along these lines can of course only be correct if the rule of law doctrine is (still) valid as outlined in the previous paragraphs. In this regard, it must be taken into account that – despite the common understanding as outlined in the previous paragraphs - the notion of legal certainty has been under attack for quite some time.[30] For the sake of establishing a transparent basis for the discussion of rule-intrinsic flexibility, arguments put forward in this regard have to be revisited in the following sections.[31] While the "underlying concepts are deceptively complex and ambiguous"[32], it must be emphasized again that it is not and it cannot be the goal of this article to dismantle all of such complexity and ambiguity. In contrast, it is the main goal of this article to expose the doctrinal context dependency of any flexibility claim.

3.1.3 Predictability and the (Potential) Indeterminacy of the Law

The debates around the viability of the notion of legal certainty are closely linked to the topic of 'legal indeterminacy', one of the main themes of the

---

[26] *Cf.* Mason (note 11) 93.
[27] *Cf.* C. Kee and E. Muñoz, "In Defence of the CISG" (2009) 14 Deakin L. Rev. 99-123,102.
[28] *Cf.* Mills (note 4) 205.
[29] *Cf.* Mason (note 11) 96; Morrison, Geary and Jago (note 11) 77; Schauer (note 25) 597.
[30] *Cf.* MacCormick 2005 (note 22) 11, 54.
[31] *Cf.* B.Z. Tamanaha, *On the Rule of Law* (Cambridge, 2004) 90, claiming that the related debate "has fizzled out".
[32] B. Bix, *Law, Language and Legal Determinacy* (Oxford 1993) 180.

American realist movement during the first half of the last century.[33] According to the realists rules are necessarily vague. Furthermore, as every legal system consists of competing rules judges have to make choices as to which rule(s) should be given priority. Depending on such decision judges may potentially reach contradicting outcomes.[34]

Representatives of the critical legal studies (CLS) movement[35] have argued along these lines on the basis that law is a result of political determinates.[36] According to CLS, judges consequently make decisions which are not determined by the law but are rather based on political choice.[37] Furthermore, such choice is guided by contradicting principles.[38] Andrew Altman has pointed out that this is not necessarily a consequence of legal indeterminacy and vice versa legal indeterminacy does not automatically imply any political determination of the law. In contrast, CLS has tr*ie*d to draw attention to the potential indeterminacy of the law to "delegitimate … [the current legal] order by undercutting that order's own conception of why it is legitimate."[39]

H.L.A. Hart acknowledged the potential uncertainty of law[40] as a result of what he called the 'open texture' of rules.[41] According to Hart,

---

33 A. Altman, "Legal Realism, Critical Studies and Dworkin" (1986) 15 Philosophy & Public Affairs 205-235 (*passim*), listing in note 4 of page 206, six distinct themes of the realist movement: (i) law as being driven by social purposes and policies, (ii) the meaning of law being assessed with a focus on the behavior of legal officials, (iii) legal indeterminacy, (iv) the call for a de-abstracting the law and rather focusing on a "very low level" with reference to the facts of particular cases, (v) private law to be understood as embodying state imposed regulatory policy, and – as a general theme that underpins all the other themes (vi) abolition of the distinction between law and politics; *cf.* G. Frankenberg, "Down by Law: Irony, Seriousness, And Reason", (1989) 83 Northwestern University Law Review, 360 – 397 (384).

34 K. Llewellyn, *The Bramble Bush* (New York 2008) 55-71; K. Llewellyn, "Some Realism About Realism" (1931) 44 Harv. L. Rev. 1222-1256, 1222, 1252-1953; F. Cohen, "The Ethical Basis of Legal Criticism" (1931) 41 Yale L. J. 201 – 220,215-219.

35 For the diversity of topics addressed by CLS *cf.* the CLS bibliography in (1984) 94 Yale L. J. 464 – 490; R. M. Unger, "The 'Critical Legal Studies Movement'" (1983) 96 Harvard L. Rev. 561 – 675; J. Hasnas, "Back to the Future: From Critical Legal Studies Forward to Legal Realism, or How Not to Miss the Point of the Indeterminacy Argument", (1995-96) Duke Law Journal 84-132; Frankenberg (note 33), 383 ("derides any attempt to develop a "unified school").

36 *Eg* Frankenberg (note 33), 362, 391; *cf.* Tamanaha 2004 (note 31), 86; K. Kress, "Legal Indeterminacy" (1977) 77 California Law Review, 283-337, 283.

37 *Cf.* the summary by Altman (note 33) 214-222, 217.

38 *Cf.* D. Kennedy, "The Political Significance of the Structure of the Law School Curriculum" (1983) 14 Seton Hall L. Rev.1- 16, 2, 16; Unger (note 35) 571; Altman (note 33) 217.

39 Altman (note 33), 217, 215 note 27; Tamanaha 2004 (note 31) 86; L.B. Solum, "On the Indeterminacy Crisis: Critiquing Critical Dogma" U. Chi. L. Rev. (1987) 54, 462-503, 463.

40 H.L.A. Hart, *The Concept of Law*, 2nd ed. (Oxford, 1994) 124-154.

> "whichever device, precedent or legislation, is chosen for the communication of standards of behaviour, these, however smoothly they work over the great mass of ordinary cases, will, at some point where their application is in question, prove indeterminate ..."[42]

Hart, however, has not regarded this as a real problem because "in the vast majority of decided cases, there is very little doubt. The headnote is usually correct enough."[43] This approach may seem practical. However, it is hardly helpful for a systematic discussion of doctrinal questions as it leaves issues unexplained. Hart[44] went even further when he regarded the open texture of legal rules as an advantage rather than a disadvantage because this allowed rules to be "interpreted reasonably when they are applied to situations and to types of problems that their authors did not foresee or could not have foreseen."[45] While according to this viewpoint rule-intrinsic flexibility is apparently an automatic consequence of any rule, it remains unclear how this corresponds with the rule of law requirement of legal certainty.

Others have pointed to the fact that "flesh-and-blood judges"[46] will not be able to meet the requirements of legal certainty. According to this viewpoint the rule of law is based on the (ideal) understanding of an impeccable judge,[47] famously called "Hercules" by Ronald Dworkin.[48] Upholding the demand for predictability as

> "a regulative idea by which judges must orient themselves if they want to do justice ... would therefore only accommodate a desire to endorse legal decisions that are in fact determined by interest positions, political attitudes, ideological biases, or other external factors."[49]

---

41 *Ibid.* 124-125; for the roots of Hart's 'open texture' approach in the works of F. Waisman and tentatively L. Wittgenstein *cf.* Bix (note 32), 7, 10-17.
42 Hart, *ibid.* 128.
43 *Ibid.* 134.
44 *Ibid.* 125-126; also *cf.* C.L. Kutz, "Just Disagreement: Indeterminacy and Rationality in the Rule of Law", (1993-1994) 103 Yale L.J., 997-1030, 1020.
45 *Cf.* Bix (note 32) 8.
46 J. Habermas, *Between Facts and Norms – Contributions to a Discourse Theory of Law and Democracy* (translated by W. Rehg) (New Baskerville 1996) 214
47 *Cf.* Altma*n* (note 33) 213, 220; Habermas (note 46) 213 ff.
48 R. Dworkin, *Taking Rights Seriously* (Cambridge 1977) 105 ff.
49 Habermas (note 46) 213-214.

Some commentators have added that "evaluative criteria"[50] relevant to answer a particular legal question or the available alternative answers may be incommensurable thus leading to an impossibility to make an objective decision.[51] Dworkin has reportedly responded to this[52] by stating that it is unproven that cases of incommensurability exist. It also needs to be kept in mind that the rule of law doctrine simply presupposes that (predictable) decisions can be made on the basis of "all things to be considered".[53] The incommensurability claim may describe problems of the application of law in action. It can, however, not challenge the rule of law as an ideal. I will return to this point later in this section.

Jürgen Habermas has questioned the notions of legal certainty and predictability on the basis that legal norms do not contain "built-in application procedures":[54]

> "(E)xcept for those norms whose "if" clauses specify application conditions in such detail that they apply only to a few highly typified and well-circumscribed standard situations (and cannot be applied elsewhere without hermeneutical difficulties), all norms are inherently indeterminate. ... Because such norms are only prima facie candidates for application, one must first enter a discourse of application to test whether they apply in a given situation."[55]

Habermas proposes to overcome related problems by way of effectively re-defining the meaning of legal certainty with reference to procedural rights.

> "Procedural rights guarantee each legal person the claim to a fair procedure that in turn guarantees not certainty of outcome but a discursive clarification of the pertinent facts and legal questions."[56]

A potential weak point of the Habermasian approach could be seen in the fact that procedural certainty and certainty vis-à-vis substantive law rule application are not identical.[57] And, it appears to be the latter that stands in the centre of

---

[50] Bix (note 33) 104.

[51] *Cf.* J. Finnis, "On Reason and Authority in *Law's Empire*" (1987) 6 Law and Philosophy 357-380 , 372-374; J. Raz, *The Morality of Freedom* (Oxford 1986), 321-366.

[52] In lectures at Oxford University, *cf.* Bix (note 33), 97; also *cf.* Kress (note 36) 335.

[53] *Cf.* Bix, *ibid.*

[54] *Ibid.* 220.

[55] *Ibid.* 217.

[56] *Ibid.* 220.

[57] *Cf.* Paunio (note 25) 1475: "... procedure is not enough to guarantee legal certainty.".

the traditional rule of law doctrine. More importantly, it is obvious that procedure itself is also based on rules. From the viewpoint of Habermas, the same predictability problems therefore arise in relation to procedural rules as in relation to substantive law rules because procedural rules do as well not provide for "built-in application procedures". [58]

Neil MacCormick in his analysis of the relationship between rhetoric and the rule of law[59] emphasizes the "arguable character" of the law:[60]

> "No less ancient than recognition of the Rule of Law as a political ideal is recognition of law's domain as a locus of argumentation, a nursery of rhetoric in all its elegant and persuasive but sometimes dubious arts.
> …
> The idea of the arguable character of law seems to pour cold water on any idea of legal certainty or security. If there can be no legal certainty, how can the Rule of Law be of such value as is claimed?"[61]

MacCormick attempts to answer his question with reference to what he calls the "dynamic aspect of the law" which is "illustrated by the rights of the defence, the importance of letting everything that is arguable be argued. In this dynamic aspect, the arguable character of law is no antithesis of the Rule of Law, but one of its components."[62] Tamanaha has added that "(w)hen ambiguities and doubts exist in a given situation of rule application, they are resolved through reasoned analysis."[63] These conclusions are convincing. They are, however, first of all concerned with legal reality and they cannot assist in

---

58 *Cf.* Habermas (note 46) 220; Paunio, (note 25) 1473; for the fact that Habermas "seeks to defend the now classic modernist vision of law as achieving social integration, channeling political participation, and subordinating power to democratic purposes", see J. Simon, "Between Power and Knowledge: Habermas, Focault, and the Future of Legal Studies" (1994) 28 Law & Society Review (No. 4) 947-961 (952); also *cf.* H. Baxter, "System and Life-World in Habermas's 'Theory of Communicative Action' ", (1987) 16 Theory and Society (No. 1) 39-86; J. B. Thomson, "Rationality and Social Rationalization: An Assessment of Habermas's Theory of Communicative Action", (1983) 17 Sociology (No. 2), 278-294; D. Abraham, "Persistant Facts and Compelling Norms: Liberal Capitalism, Democratic Socialism, and the Law", (1994) 28 Law & Society Review (No. 4), 939-946; J. L. Staats, "The Threat to Democracy of Unchecked Corporate Power", (2004) 57 Political Research Quarterly (No. 4) (2004) 585-594.

59 MacCormic*k* 1993 (note 22); also *cf.* N. MacCormick, "Rhetoric and the Rule of Law" in D. Dyzenhaus (ed), *Recrafting the Rule of Law: The Limits of Legal Order* (Oxford/Portland, 1999), 163-177.

60 MacCormick 1993 (note 22) 13; also *cf.* MacCormick 1999 (note 59) 163-177; J. Waldron, "The Concept and the Rule of Law" (2008) 43 Ga. L. Rev. 1-61.

61 MacCormick 1993 (note 22) 13.

62 *Ibid.* 31.

63 Tamanaha 2004 (note 31) 88.

dissolving the potential contradiction between legal certainty and rule-inherent flexibility from the viewpoint of legal doctrine. In other words these conclusions are unable to answer the question if the rule of law doctrine permits flexible rules.

Many of the above-quoted authors have of course developed their positions on the basis of and in differentiating themselves from the Dworkinian point of view.[64] In his celebrated and at the same time often criticized works Ronald Dworkin has concluded that a situation, in which the law does not provide an answer to any legal question, cannot exist. He argued that the legal system consists of rules as well as of standards other than rules. According to Dworkin rules and standards always offer authoritative and predictable guidance in relation to legal questions.[65]

This article is based on the traditional understanding of the rule of law doctrine[66] and will therefore not adopt the arguments and opinions of the critics of the notion of legal certainty as outlined in the previous paragraphs. The reasons for my approach are as follows:

First of all, it appears that the traditional understanding of the rule of law still represents the prevailing opinion among legal practitioners and scholars. In particular, those who argue in favour of flexibility have - as far as I can see - not indicated any deviation from such traditional understanding. Secondly, as mentioned earlier[67], legal certainty is a centre pillar of the rule of law doctrine. Dismissing the notion of legal certainty would therefore affect the rule of law doctrine at its core and nobody has convincingly explained why and how this could be justifiable. Thirdly, I believe for the following reasons that the notion of legal certainty as embodied by the traditional rule of law doctrine remains unaffected by the criticism of those who point to any potential indeterminacy of the law.

---

64 *Cf.* Bix (note 32), 78.

65 *Cf.* R. Dworkin, "Judicial Discretion" (1963) 60 Journal of Philosophy No. 21 624-638, 634 ff.; Dworkin 1977 (note 48) 31 ff.; R. Dworkin, "Social Rules and Legal Theory" (1971-1972) 81 Yale L. J. 855-890; *cf.* R. Sartorius, 'Social Policy and Judicial Legislation' (1971) 8 Am Phil. Q. (No. 2), 151-160; *cf.* B. Hoffmaster, Understanding Judicial Discretion, 1 Law and Philosophy (1982), 21-55 (34, 37), claiming that Dworkin "has not shown that whenever legal rules fail to provide authoritative guidance for a judge, there will always be binding legal principles to fill the void."

66 *Supra*, 3.1.1 and 3.1.2.

67 *Ibid.*

It is in the very nature of law that decisions must be made[68] , *ie* "authority is basic to the nature of law."[69] Moreover, it is the postulate of the law that these decisions must (ideally) be the uniquely correct ones because legal assertions are always normative in nature and it is imperative that they have to lay claim to correctness. In contrast, accepting that there can be more than one answer to a legal question would lead to arbitrariness and deceive the whole idea of the law determining what is right and what is wrong.

I believe that Dworkin was right in saying that the legal system comprises not just rules, but also other binding legal standards[70] that must be taken into account when making decisions. These rules and other standards always allow for correct answers to each legal question on the basis of all the concerned interests and relevant facts.[71] It may of course not always be possible to identify the uniquely correct answer by way of logical deduction e.g. from precedents or statutory rules. In contrast, it will almost always be necessary to evaluate the different factors relevant for a decision and to balance them against each other. And, under the rule of law there can only be one correct way how such balancing is to be done. Law cannot be indeterminate.

It is, however, also important to remember that the rule of law is an ideal.[72] As such the rule of law serves as benchmark against which legal decisions, theories and arguments must be assessed.[73] Many authors have pointed out that in practice things are much more complicated than any doctrine may ever be able to suggest.[74] In fact, the indeterminacy thesis focuses on practice, more

---

[68] MacCormick 1993 (note 22) 2; Altman (note 33) 220; *cf.* Perelman (note 6) 39; Kress (note 36), 335

[69] Bix (note 32), 183.

[70] The term "binding legal standards" is used here to avoid the - in the context of this article unnecessary - discussion of the existence and nature of different elements and propositions of a legal system; *cf.*, however, *Dworkin* 1977 (note 45) 31; B. Simpson, "The Common Law and Legal Theory" in W. Twining (ed.), *Legal Theory and Common Law* (Oxford and New York, 1986) 8-25, 9 and *passim.*

[71] *Cf.* Sartorius (note 65) 158; Stammler, (note 18), 98, 105.

[72] Stein (note 22) 303; also *cf.* N. Lacey, The Jurisprudence of Discretion: Escaping the Legal Paradigm, in Keith Hawkins (ed.) *The Uses of Discretion* (Clarendon Press, Oxford, 1992) 361-388, 369; MacCormick 2005 (note 23) 3, 23, 27; H.L.A Hart, "American Jurisprudence Through English Eyes: The Nightmare and the Noble Dream" (1977) 11 Ga L. Rev. 969-989 978 ff.; Habermas 1996 (note 46) 213, referring to Dworkin ("postulated theory of this sort in the grip of strong idealization"); Simpson (note 70) 24.

[73] MacCormick 2005 (note 23) 12: "The Rule of Law is a signal virtue in civilized societies."

[74] *Cf.* T. D. Perry, "Judicial Method and the Concept of Reasoning" (1969) 80 Ethics 1-20, 6: " … there can be no way to identify the uniquely correct or best decision, and … there is very little point in even speaking of such a decision in such case."; Bix (note 32), 119; the criticism of K. Greenawalt, "Discretion and Judicial Decision: The Elusive Quest for the Fetters that Bind

precisely on court practice.[75] The discrepancies between law and legal reality must, however, be regarded as shortfalls of legal practice which fails to meet the ideal requirements of the rule of law doctrine.[76] The rule of law cannot be affected by this as it is the rule of law which sets the standards for legal practice and not the other way round.[77]

3.1.4 Consolidating Legal Certainty and Flexibility?

The discussion in the previous chapter was necessary to reconfirm that legal certainty as required under the rule of law doctrine still needs to be considered when exploring the legal significance of flexibility. The question to be answered in the following therefore is whether there is any room for flexible rules in a rule of law-based system. In other words, one must contemplate whether legal certainty and flexibility can co-exist.

As already mentioned, unfortunately, calls for flexibility and arguments that are based on flexibility claims are normally not supported by comprehensive explanations regarding the relationship between flexibility and the rule of law. The existence of any contradiction between the rule of law on the hand and flexibility on the other hand is often not even acknowledged. On the contrary, it seems that flexibility claims are made whenever this seems to help a certain cause without deeper reflection.[78] Attempts to overcome the dichotomy between the rule of law and flexibility are rare and - at the most - tacit. Many authors have e.g. tried to bypass the problem by emphasizing varying degrees of legal certainty and flexibility. For example, it has been said that "some degree

Judges", (1975) 75 Columbia Law Review, pp. 360-399 (386), that "(d)iscretion exists so long as not practical procedure exists for determining if a result is correct, informed lawyers disagree about the proper result, and a judge's decision either way will not widely be considered a failure to perform his judicial responsibilities", is therefore only correct to the extent that discretion is understood as a description of judicial decision making in practice rather than in the context of legal doctrine.

[75] Tamanaha 2004 (note 31) 86.

[76] Sartorius (note 65) 159: "The theoretical possibility of the law being indeterminate with regard to what it requires, in other words, does not imply any corresponding indeterminacy with regard to what is required from a judge."; *cf.* Hart 1977 (note 72), reporting on Dworkin's theory at 983: "... the judge ... is never to determine what the law shall be; he is confined to saying what he believes *is* the law before his decision, though of course he may be mistaken. ... He must not suppose that the law is ever incomplete, inconsistent, or indeterminate; if it appears so, the fault is not in *it*, but in the judge's limited human powers of discernment, so there is no space of a judge to make law by choosing between alternatives as to what shall be the law."

[77] *Cf.* Hart 1977 (note 72) 981, discussing R. Pound's position ("a regulative ideal for judges to pursue").

[78] *Cf.* Harris (note 6) 381.

of certainty, predictability, and … 'fairness' are required, within even a flexible regime of substantive rules."[79]

The reference to degrees of flexibility is, however, misleading. This is because the relationship between legal certainty and flexibility is a mutually exclusive one. Either there is legal certainty or there is rule-inherent flexibility. It is logically impossible to allow both at the same time,[80] as legal certainty will necessarily disappear with the introduction of the tiniest element of flexibility. Moreover, allowing degrees of flexibility would in practice require the quantification of those degrees of flexibility that are allowable. And such quantification would be practically impossible. It also follows that the often-quoted tension between flexibility and legal certainty[81] does simply not exist. In fact, it cannot exist. Legal rules are either flexible or they provide for legal certainty. Rule-inherent flexibility is nothing else but an oxymoron.

3.1.5 Can only Flexibility Lead to Justice in Individual Cases?

It was the conclusion of the previous chapters that rules which contain elements of flexibility are not permissible within a rule of law-based system. What needs to be considered now is how these findings correspond with the claim[82] that only flexibility can lead to justice in individual cases.[83]

This claim is of course necessarily based on the implied assumption that justice cannot be achieved within a system that mandates predictability. In light of the

79 Chibundu, (note 20), 88-89; *cf.* J D Heydon, "How Far Can Trial Courts and Intermediate Appellate Courts Develop the Law?" (2009) 9 Oxford University Commonwealth Law Journal 1-46, 10: "The courts accept that while certainty is not always attainable, a measure of predictability is."; Lord Bingham (note 22) para. 16; Atiyah and Summers (note 9), 410; W Twining/D Miers, How To Do Things with Rules, 4th ed. (London/Edinburgh/Dublin: Butterworths, 1999), 180: "… some choice, but the range of possible or plausible or otherwise appropriate interpretations is in practice subject to constraints."; Mason, (note 11) 95: "The tension between the desire for consistency and predictability on the one hand and the desire for adaptability and justice in the particular case presents a problem for precedent. It calls for a doctrine sufficiently flexible and elastic to enable the courts to share the best of these inconsistent worlds."; Harris (note 6) 355 ("element of flexibility"); MacCormick 2005 (note 23) 12 ("reasonable predictability").

80 Critical Kirby (note 11) 23: "… the principles work well, taken as a whole. They give measure of stability and predictability to the law without imposing hidebound inflexibility."; also *cf.* from the viewpoint of indeterminacy of the law Tamanaha 31(note 31) 87, 89; Kress (note 36), 295-336.

81 *Cf.* Mason (note 11) 96; Morrison,Geary and Jago (note 11) 77.

82 *Supra,*chapter 2.

83 C. E. Schneider, "Discretion and Rules – A Lawyer's View" in *Hawkins* (n 53) 47-88, 56, 63; *cf.* Mason (note 11) 94.

discussion in the previous chapters it is obvious that this assumption is unjustified. Within the realm of the rule of law ideal the law always provides for the uniquely correct answer to a particular legal question[84] and such answer must be the answer that achieves justice in the sense that all concerned interests and facts are taken into account and be given the appropriate weight.[85] Consequently, flexibility is not at all required to achieve justice in a system that mandates predictability. On the contrary, it is rule-inherent flexibility that must be regarded as an obstacle to justice because rule-inherent flexibility would necessarily make more than one solution available, thus rendering legal certainty unachievable.

3.2 The Flexible Application of the Law

Some authors have directly or indirectly drawn attention to the fact that flexibility may be a feature of judicial practice, *ie* of the application of the law.[86] This article is not meant to analyze the empirical reality of court practice with the goal to explore if rules are applied in a flexible manner.[87] What is important, however, is to consider if the flexible application of the law can be justifiable from the viewpoint of the rule of law. The above conclusions pave the way for a straight forward answer.

If, as demonstrated[88], there cannot be a proper rule that allows for flexibility, then there can as well not be a flexible application of the law that is proper. This is because the flexible application of any legal rule would necessarily imply a deviation from such rule because the rule itself does not provide for the way in which it is applied. Courts which apply rules in a flexible manner therefore fail to apply rules as they are set, in other words they fail to abide by the law.

---

[84] *Supra,* chapters 3.1.3 and 3.1.4.

[85] *Cf.* Hart 1977 (note 72) 979; R. Pound, "The Theory of Judicial Decision" (1923) 36 Harvard L. Rev. 641-662.

[86] *Cf. supra,* chapter 2; Donaldson J.in *Corocraft Ltd v Pan American Airways Inc.* [1969] 1 Q.B. 622 at 638: "… the judges do not act as computers into which are fed the statutes and the rules for the construction of statutes and from whom issue forth the mathematically correct answer. The interpretation of statutes is a craft as much as a science and the judges, as craftsmen, select and apply the appropriate rules as the tools of their trade. …".

[87] *Cf. eg* C. Manchester and D. Salter, *Exploring the Law: The Dynamics of Precedent and Statutory Interpretation*, 3rd ed. (London 2006) 48; Lord Reid in *Maunsell v Olins* [1975] A.C. 373 at 382; I. McLeod, Legal Method 7th ed. (Hampshire/New York: Palgrave Macmillan, 2009), 282: "… whether it is sensible to speak of 'rules' of interpretation at all. You may well conclude that the word 'rules' implies a degree of rigidity and precision, and therefore a predictability of outcome, which is simply not present in practice."; Whytock (note 23), 735-736.

[88] *Supra,* chapter 3.1.3.

The flexible application of the law would therefore be illegal in the best sense of the word.

3.3 The Flexibility of the Common Law

It has been claimed that flexibility is a special attribute of the common law. Scarman J.'s statement in this regard in *McLoughlin v O'Brien*[89] was already quoted above.[90] In *Dietrich v* R[91] Justice Brennan added that the "Common Law has been created by the Courts and the genius of the Common Law system consists in the ability of the Courts to mould the law to correspond with the contemporary values of society."

Schneider[92] has argued along these lines when emphasizing that "despite the doctrine of stare decisis … judges often have real discretion in shaping and reshaping legal doctrines. Common-law decision-making seems not just designed to secure doctrinal flexibility. It also conduces to allowing judges to 'do justice' in a particular case where a rule seems not to."

Under the model developed in the previous chapters these conclusions are not sustainable. As long as the common law is rule of law-based flexible rules should not be allowable.[93] The flexible application of common law rules is not possible either.[94] Flexibility can therefore only be a common law feature if one is willing to accept that the common law is not rule of law-based or that the rule of law concept does not require legal certainty.[95] The latter would strip the rule of law concept of one of its core contents.

3.4 The Flexibility of Case Law

Case law[96] has sometimes been regarded as more flexible than statutory law.[97] Again, the conclusions of the previous chapters cast doubt on the correctness

---

89 *McLoughlin v. O'Brien* [1983] 1 AC 410.
90 *Supra,* chapter 2.
91 [1992] 109 ALR 385, 402 f.
92 Schneider (note 83) 56-57.
93 *Supra,* chapters 3.1.3 and 3.1.4.
94 *Supra,* chapter 3.2.
95 For the potential flexibility of case law *cf. infra,* chapter 3.4.
96 For the fact that according to modern comparative law theory the source(s) of the law can only to a limited extent be a distinguishing feature of a legal system, *cf.* K. Zweigert/H. Kötz, An Introduction to Comparative Law, 3rd ed. – translated by Tony Weir (Oxford: Clarendon Press, 1998), 71.

of this assumption, at least as far as existing law is concerned. The rule of law doctrine requires judges to identify and apply the law in its uniquely correct form. There is no room for flexibility and it does not make any difference whether the law to be applied is case-based or not.

Interestingly, flexibility can, however, be an issue in relation to case law insofar as case law is to be regarded as the creation of new law[98] rather than just a formulation of what already exists.[99] Law making activities of judges are not free-standing, but have to be conducted within specific frameworks. Judges have to follow procedural rules when making decisions.[100] In this regard judge-made law is predictable and thus not flexible. As for the substance of case law, judges are bound by the broader framework of the constitution.[101] To the extent that case law cannot be unconstitutional, law making activities of judges would therefore again be in line with the understanding developed in the previous chapters, *ie* there cannot be any flexibility.

Law making activities of judges are, however, not subject to a requirement of absolute predictability. In contrast, judges are not "legally required to approve one kind of legislation rather than another, at least in the absence of constitutional restraints."[102] In other words, the rule of law doctrine does not extend the requirement of predictability to law yet to be enacted. In this regard, judges do therefore seem to have flexibility when making new law. This kind of flexibility is, however, not a feature that distinguishes case law from statutory law. In contrast, judge-made law and the law enacted by other law-making bodies should be exactly the same from this point of view.[103] Moreover, it must be remembered that all this is based on the proposition that judges do in fact

---

[97] *Lord Wilberforce* (note 7); *cf.* Morrison/Geary/Jago (note 11) 72 stating that codification has not become the solution to "the problem of a perceived chaos of competing cases and seemingly ad hoc, if not retrospective judicial 'law making' ".

[98] *Cf.* Lord Reid, "The Judge as Law Maker" (1972) 12 Journal of the Society of Public Teachers 22-29; M.H. McHugh, "The Judicial Method" http://www.hcourt.gov.au/speeches/mchughj/mchughj_london1.htm > accessed 30 May 2010.

[99] *Cf.* Dworkin 1963 (note 65), 638; Dworkin 1977 (note 48), 84; *Kleinwort Benson* v. *Lincoln City* [1998] 3 WLR 1095.

[100] *Cf.* R.S. Summers, "How Law is Formal and Why it Matters" (1997) 82 Cornell Law Review 1156-1229, 1212 (reprinted in R.S. Summers, *The Jurisprudence of Law's Form and Substance* (Aldershot 2000), 37-101).

[101] See *Duport Steels Ltd v Sirs* [1980] 1 All ER 529 per Lord Scarman; *Lord Bingham* (note 22), from the viewpoint of *nulla poena, sine legem.*

[102] Greenawalt (note 74) 372.

[103] One difference between judge-made law and law created via parliamentary acts would, however, be the fact that judges create law for immediate application.

create new law. The declaratory theory, although no longer *en vogue*, dismisses this idea altogether.

3.5 The Flexible Form of Rules

Finally, flexibility has been identified as a feature of the form that legal rules can take.[104] As already mentioned[105], Robert S. Summers and P.S. Atiyah have described "flexible rules" as rules which "grant discretion with or without standards for its exercise, or [incorporation of] vague concepts such as 'reasonableness'".[106] Summers and Attiyah distinguish this type of rules from what they have called "hard and fast rules" with high authoritative formality, high content formality, total mandatory formality and strict interpretive formality.[107]

To the extent that this characterization only relates to the form[108] of rules the term "flexible rules" differs from what has been discussed in the previous sections of this article. This is because the open form of a rule does not necessarily imply openness also in terms of substance.[109] As suggested by Summers' and Atiyah's above definition of "flexible rules", the form of a rule which itself does not provide for standards for the exercise of discretion may be described as open. These standards may, however, be available outside such rule, e.g. on the basis of general principles. Similarly, methodological tools may be available to interpret any vague concepts of a rule. In both cases the respective rule itself may take an open form while at the same time the contents of such rule would be determinable. The rule would therefore not be open-ended in terms of contents and the problem of legal certainty as discussed in the previous sections of this article would not arise.

Summers has, however, demonstrated how form and substance of rules are interrelated.[110] In fact, a rule could grant discretion without any standards for its exercise being available at all. And, a rule could incorporate vague concepts without access to any methodological tools for the interpretation of such

---

104 Summers 1997 (note 100), 1176; also *cf.* R.S. Summers, "The Formal Character of Law" (1992) 51 Cambridge L.J. 242-262.
105 *Supra,* chapter 2.
106 Atiyah and Summers (note 9), 71-88; also *cf.* Summers 1992 (note 104), 245-246.
107 *Ibid.*
108 Note that according to Summers 1992 (note 104), 1169, note 6, the typology of form used by him differs from the one used in the book he has published together with Atiyah (note 9).
109 *Cf.* Summers 1992 (note 104), 242.
110 Summers 1992 (note 104), 88-89, 94, 97, 246, 259.

concepts. In both scenarios, not only the form of the respective rules would be open, but also their contents. An example provided by Summers makes this point clearer: "A 65mph rule shapes form and content differently than a 'drive reasonably' rule."[111] The form of the latter is not definite and could be called "flexible". The question whether the 'drive reasonably' rule carries rule-intrinsic flexibility depends, however, on the availability of a definite interpretation of the word 'reasonable'. Where such a definite interpretation is not available the substance of the rule would be open-ended and the respective rule would in fact carry intrinsic flexibility with all the rule of law-implications discussed in the previous sections.

4. Summary and Final Remarks

While often used in legal discourse, no common definition of the term 'flexibility' exists. In contrast, reference to 'flexibility' is made in a variety of ways and in relation to different aspects, usually without the provision of evidence of its existence and often perhaps without much reflection. It was the main goal of this article to draw attention to the limits of flexibility imposed by the rule of law.

In the legal context flexibility entails uncertainty. Based on the acknowledgement that this is not in line with the (traditional) rule of law doctrine one has to conclude that flexibility should not be an inherent element of any legal rule, it should not be a predicate of the application of legal rules and it cannot be a distinguishing feature of the Common Law compared with other legal traditions unless one is prepared to reconsider the rule of law doctrine altogether.

Many aspects of the traditional rule of law model have been subject to sometimes fierce criticism. As far as the legal (in)significance of flexibility is concerned, such criticism could indeed lead to conclusions which differ substantially from those developed in this article. However, to achieve argumentative sustainability any deviation from the traditional understanding of the rule of law doctrine would require a thoroughly established and explained doctrinal basis. In contrast, any flexibility claim without a clear definition of this term and without an explanation of related reference systems is no more than a rhetorical silver bullet which is as useless as a projectile that gets stuck in the gun barrel for good.

111 *Ibid.*

REPUBLICAN FREEDOM: THREE PROBLEMS

John A. Bruegger, J.D., LL.M.[1]

The concept of civic republican freedom has been described as a third alternative to the negative concept of liberty espoused by scholars from John Locke to Ian Carter and the positive liberty of self-mastery associated with the neo-Hegelians.[2] However, throughout the numerous scholarly discussions of modern republicanism, three troublesome issues arise for which no answer has sufficiently been provided. First, if the concepts of interference and domination are defined in such a way that the focus is shifted from the modern negative view of liberty as non-interference to the republican view of liberty as non-domination, a situation arises where the state now has the power to interfere in the lives of its citizens without reducing freedom *ex hypothesi*, as long as it is careful to ensure that the interference is "non-arbitrary." Secondly, to maintain this definition of freedom, certain protections are needed to keep the government, armed with the power to impose interference that by definition will not reduce liberty, from running amok and dominating the citizens. Finally, even in a state where the government does not dominate, and where any interference, to the extent it is imposed, is non-arbitrary, the citizens are not really "free" from domination – they are just "free for now" – if the citizens do not risk unfreedom from their own government, those citizens live constantly under the possibility of domination by another more powerful state or coalition of states.

The purpose of this article is to discuss each of these three troublesome issues and thoroughly examine the logical conclusions of modern republican freedom theory. Although I do not allege herein that these criticisms are the only ones

---

[1] J.S.D. Candidate, Washington University in St. Louis, School of Law; LL.M., Taxation (2006), Washington University in St. Louis, School of Law; J.D. (2001), Saint Louis University School of Law; B.A. (1998), University of Missouri. The author is incredibly grateful to Professor Brian Z. Tamanaha at Washington University in St. Louis for his guidance and commentary on previous drafts of this article.

[2] Pettit, Philip. *Republicanism: A Theory of Freedom and Government.* Oxford: Oxford University Press (1997), pages 19, 21. For purposes of this Article, I will associate the modern negative view of liberty with those roughly described by Hillel Steiner, Ian Carter and Matthew Kramer. Although there are important differences in the negative liberty espoused by each of these writers, those differences will not be relevant for my purposes here.

possible against the civic republican theory, they must be properly considered to properly understand and evaluate republican liberty theory.[3]

I. The Dangerous Distinction Between Interference and Domination.

A. Interference and Domination – A Difference of Focus.

The fundamental difference between modern negative liberty and republican liberty centers on how one's liberty is restricted. According to negative liberty theorists, interference or coercion is required for the restriction or lessening of one's liberty. As Isaiah Berlin states, "I am normally said to be free to the degree to which no man or body of men interferes with my activity."[4] Republicans recognize the concept of interference, but argue the negative theorists' reliance on it is misplaced. According to Philip Pettit, it is the ability of one person to *dominate* over another person that holds the key to controlling freedom:

> Domination, as I understand it here, is exemplified by the relationship of a master to slave or master to servant. Such a relationship means, at the limit, that the dominating party can interfere on an arbitrary basis with the choices of the dominated: can interfere in particular in the basis of an interest or an opinion that need not be shared by the person affected.[5]

Republicanism holds that such domination can occur in the absence of actual interference, and conversely, that interference can occur in the absence of domination.

Therefore, the main difference between the modern negative and republican theories of liberty can be, somewhat simplistically, narrowed down to a classification of the role that interference plays in the lives of the citizens. Again, for writers like Jeremy Bentham and John Stuart Mill, any law was an evil that resulted in a reduction of liberty, even if the end-result of the law was to increase a person's overall liberty. Thus, freedom exists to the extent that there is "non-interference." Republicans recognize that some law is needed for civil society to exist – although negative theorists certainly acknowledge this

---

[3] For additional viewpoints on the civic republican theories of Quentin Skinner and Philip Pettit, see Kramer, Matthew. *The Quality of Freedom.* Oxford: Oxford University Press (2008). Paperback edition. pp. 91-149.

[4] Berlin, Isaiah. "Two Concepts of Liberty" reprinted in *Liberty.* Henry Hardy, ed. Oxford: Oxford University Press (2008), page 169.

[5] Pettit (1997), page 22.

point as well. Republicans have not so much realized that some law is necessary to live in society or forced a concession from the liberals on this point, but rather they have latched on to this notion as the catapult for what will be the enormous conceptual boulder they are about to release. Most negative liberty theorists agree that some interference is necessary, and take it for what it is – a necessary evil that could (or should, if it is formed properly) lead to greater overall freedom on balance. Republicans recast interference as something else, something positive, and use that new concept of law to propagate the idea that states should only interfere in the lives of its citizens for their own good. The remainder of this section will be devoted to flushing out the major consequences of this argument.

As I stated earlier, interference occurs when a person or group A takes some action with respect to person or group B that results in the performance (or forbearance of performance) of some action by B against B's will. Interference includes physical coercion (as in restraining or obstructing the person), coercion of the will (as in punishment or the threat of punishment), and manipulation (as in misrepresenting certain facts).[6] While this would be enough for many liberals to decry their loss of freedom, republicans argue this interference occurs without a loss of liberty when the interference is not "arbitrary" – "when it is controlled by the interests and opinions of those affected, being required to serve those interests in a way that conforms with those opinions."[7] Thus, arbitrary interference is an act perpetrated without reference to the interests and opinions of those affected.[8] The choices made by A are not forced to track what the interests of B require according B's own judgments.[9] Interference is "non-arbitrary" to the extent that it is forced to track the interests and ideas of B, or at least forced to track the relevant ones.[10] This non-arbitrary interference does not compromise freedom, but merely conditions it – "If it is nonarbitrary, it won't compromise or undermine my freedom in the manner of a dominating agency, but it will offend against it in a secondary manner."[11]

While negative liberty theorists view interference as a *per se* violation of liberty, republicans view interference only as such a violation if it is "arbitrary," i.e., does not take into consideration the interests and opinions over whom the

[6] Pettit (1997), page 53.
[7] Pettit (1997), page 35.
[8] Pettit (1997), page 55.
[9] *Id.*
[10] *Id.*
[11] Pettit, Philip (2002). "Keeping Republic Freedom Simple – On a Difference With Quentin Skinner." *Political Theory*. Volume 30, No. 3, pages 339-356.

interference is imposed. What does arbitrary interference lead to? This is the second great evil in the republican theory of freedom – "domination."

Domination occurs when one person or group has the power to arbitrarily interfere in the lives of another person or group.[12] Specifically, according to the theory, person A can be considered to have dominating power over person B to the extent that (1) A has the capacity to interfere (2) on an arbitrary basis (3) in certain choices that B is in a position to make.[13] This domination of one over another causes two major problems, namely (1) it creates uncertainty in the victim of the domination, who is subject to the arbitrary interference of another, and thus, can never be sure of where he or she stands or what to expect, and relatedly (2) domination introduces an asymmetry of status, where it becomes common knowledge that the victim is exposed to the possibility of arbitrary interference.[14] The victim is uncertain as to whether, or when, he will suffer some random arbitrary interference, and because of that (and because others in society will presumably be aware of this) the victim cannot effectively command the respect and attention of others.[15] Freedom, therefore, is a freedom of "non-domination."[16]

To sufficiently drive this point home, Pettit uses the examples of criminal law and taxation to clarify what he means by arbitrary (and hence dominating) versus non-arbitrary interference.[17] Taxes are clearly a form of interference and coercion. To the extent that I no longer have a certain sum of money than I otherwise would have, I have suffered interference, and my range of choices of what to do with my money has changed against my will. Adherents to the republican liberty theory hold if we assume that the tax laws were made by the legislators in a system that tracks the relevant interests and opinions, and the tax laws were made with those opinions and interests in mind, then the tax laws are by definition not arbitrary. If they are not arbitrary, they do not dominate over

---

12 Pettit (1997), page 52.
13 *Id.*
14 Pettit (2002).
15 *Id.*
16 In his later work, Pettit describes this as "freedom of choice" and "freedom from alien control," which requires (1) the absence of alien control, not just interference, and (2) the systematic protection and empowerment against alien control over selected choices. Pettit, Philip (2008). "Law and Liberty." Reproduced in *Law and Republicanism*. Samantha Besson and Jose Luis Marti, eds. Oxford: Oxford University Press (forthcoming), retrieved from http://www.ssrn.com/abstract=1281157. However, this is really only a nomenclature change, as Pettit exchanges "domination" for "alien control." Furthermore, the "systematic protection" discussed under (2) are addressed later in this article, so there is no need to further address it here.
17 Pettit (1997), page 55.

the citizens. Liberals may consider it a reduction in freedom, outweighed by the benefits that tax dollars mean to overall freedom, such as public provision for the military, schools, roads, and so on, but taxes are freedom-reducing nonetheless. Republicans, on the other hand, would not consider taxes to be freedom-reducing (again, assuming the non-arbitrariness condition is met).

There is also a dual personality that citizens exhibit when it comes to the laws, and I believe this dual personality can be separated as (1) me, as an individual, versus (2) me, as an indivisible member of an overall society. Thus, I, as the member of society, understand the benefits of imposing a set of criminal laws on society, such that individuals who are properly convicted of such crimes are made to suffer a particular punishment. Furthermore, I, as a member of society, understand the tremendous usefulness that a proper system of taxes plays in the financing of necessary state functions, such as security, healthcare, education, building infrastructure, and so forth. However, my other personality, the I-as-an-individual, cringes when I get my tax bill. I would rather not pay it, because I would rather use that money for something else. Even if I have an important use for that money, a use that means far more to me than an intangible social goal of generalized healthcare or education, such as buying medicine for my sick child, I am forced to use that money to pay my taxes instead or suffer negative consequences. In my individual capacity, I do not really want to pay taxes – or at least I am less than enthusiastic about doing so. Similarly, if I suddenly find myself charged with some crime, whether it is a minor traffic offense or a serious felony, I do not wish to be punished as harshly as provided by the law.

In both of the situations described above, I have conflicting interests, because I have conflicting personalities, at least on some level. Where the individual interest conflicts with the societal or group interest, according to civic republicanism, the state is required only to track the interests and opinions of the group.[18] In the battle between individual and group, the group interest wins.

B. Problem #1 – Legislating "For Your Own Good" and Calling it Freedom.

The republican form of freedom opens the door for the state to legislate on behalf of the people, against the people's individual goals, wishes and desires, as long as the state can claim some higher "group" or societal good that it has taken into account. "Freedom" in this sense is not lessened by any number of

[18] *Id.*

paternalistic laws that may be quite oppressive or interfering in the lives of the people, as long as the state's conception of what is in the best interest of the group is taken into account. In this manner, the republican state can force you to be free.[19]

How can this be so? Consider two reasonable assumptions: (1) first, that any law passed by democratic means will not have support of 100% of the people to which it will apply, for even laws with a super-majority support still has some dissenters, and (2) laws are made to govern all of the people, not just the majority of people that voted in its favor. Clearly, if 100% support were required, no law would ever pass, or only very few. Furthermore, if a law is passed based on some method of majority rule, then clearly it must apply to some people who did not vote for it. So a citizen may still be subject to coercion of a law passed over his or her objection.

However, if we are to avoid arbitrariness in the law, and thus a law that is dominating over the people, the opinions and desires of the people must be considered. Which opinions and desires, and of which people? We have established that laws can be passed without 100% support, yet still apply to 100% of the people, the state must consider the good of the people when creating laws that all or some of the people do not desire. As in the case of taxes or the criminal law, if in my role as a citizen of the republic, a certain law is in my interest (e.g., that people pay taxes to provide for the common defense, that criminals should be punished) it is not arbitrary, and therefore does not have a dominating effect over me. This remains true in the case where, perhaps in my role as an individual selfish person, I do not want to pay taxes, or I wish to steal with impunity. My individual interests are in conflict with my interests as a citizen of the republic, and in that situation, the state need only consider my "relevant" interests, i.e., my group interests. This renders the law that is against my individual selfish will "non-arbitrary" and non-freedom-reducing.

The major problem with this is the potential for the majoritarian government to impose harsh, drastic, and severely oppressive interference on the minority opposition over their objections. The "tyranny of the majority" is inescapable in a civic republican system. Assume a society in which the majority of citizens ascribe to ideology A, and the minority ascribes to ideology B. For the sake of this assumption, we will say that 51% of the population is in A and 49% are in B. In this society, all proposed laws are drafted and put to a vote, a popular referendum, once a year. This year, there are several laws up for vote that severely restrict the activities of those people in group B. They are not allowed

[19] Rousseau, Jean-Jacques. *The Social Contract.*

to work in any employment they choose, but only must work in the most demeaning and lowest-paying jobs. Group B is not allowed to preach its message. As a matter of fact, those in group A feel that most of the beliefs and activities that define group B as a collection of people are immoral and bad for society overall.

Leaving any constitutional issues aside for now, what is the state to do? A majority, 51%, votes for the laws that severely interfere in the lives of the people who belong in group B. But, taking into account the individual opinions and desires of everyone in society as a collective group, the majority view wins, and therefore the state would be justified in enacting the harsh legislation. While it may conflict with the individual opinions and wants of those people in group B, their individual needs are overridden by what has been determined as the best overall course of action for the state. The laws, even as they apply to group B, are non-arbitrary, and therefore do not result in a loss of freedom.

Clearly the laws would be very oppressive and interfering in the lives of members of group B. The laws seem to be in the best interests (at least in their minds) of group A, so they are non-dominating and do not reduce freedom. However, those laws are clearly not in the best interest of group B as a whole, and taking the whole of their wants and opinions into account, the laws would be arbitrary and dominating.[20] Thus, these laws should not apply to group B. This solution is unworkable, because the laws would pass to restrict the activities of group B, for the sake of all the perceived benefits of such laws according to the wants and desires of group A, but then the laws would not actually apply to group B because, taking group B's wants and opinions into account, the laws are dominating. This situation quickly turns chaotic as we realize that society is made up of a real multitude of groups and sub groups, some with common interests, and some with divergent interests, and any one person can be a member of groups that both want and do not want a law to pass.

The only logical, and workable, solution is to release the "tyranny of the majority" on society and then try to institute numerous checks and controls to

[20] This is, of course, assuming that when we speak of taking the group wants and opinions into account, we mean that we determine whether the proposed law would be in the group's best interest. Modern republican freedom does not go this far in the analysis. Pettit speaks only of taking into account the relevant wants and opinions of each person. This raises the question, although I will not pursue it farther, of whether the state need only be aware of the wants and opinions of the people and incorporate them into the deliberation, without actually being committed to doing what it is in the best interest of the people as a whole.

make sure the majority cannot become too dominating of a force. Pettit certainly recognizes this result, as he proposes the controls that I will discuss in the next section. His main point seems to be to introduce the concept of domination, which can occur in the presence or absence of interference. Domination can result from the state imposing arbitrary laws, or even from just having the power to impose arbitrary laws. By re-focusing the attention on domination, instead of interference, Pettit takes this into account. However, a perhaps unintended result is that he must account for interference that does not result in domination. Thus, he proposes the arbitrary vs. non-arbitrary distinction.

This distinction is unnecessary and dangerous, as it now sets up the possibility of interference without counting it against freedom. Another alternative Pettit could have chosen was to just introduce the concept that interference and the possibility of interference both reduce freedom. By defining non-arbitrary interference as non-freedom-reducing interference, the state can now interfere without reducing freedom by definition. This leads to the possibility of the state imposing harsh interference, but not reducing the freedom of the individuals, as long as the state can justifiably argue that such interference is in the best interests of the people, or at least the majority.

II. Constitutional Limitations and Contestability are Insufficient Controls.

The inevitable conclusion of the preceding section is that by making "arbitrary interference" and "domination" the focus of freedom, the majority can interfere severely and oppressively into the lives of the minority, without calling it domination and without considering it a reduction in freedom. Since republican freedom gives the state broad power to interfere in the lives of its citizens without claiming to reduce freedom, the next task is to examine the constraints and controls modern republican theory puts in place to control for the majority domination. Pettit proposes two steps (1) constitutional (written or unwritten) limitations on the power of the state; and (2) a system where all government rules, activities, and laws are subject to the power of the people to contest such action ("contestability").[21] As shown in this section, these limits are conceptually insufficient to prevent the state from exercising its "collective will" over the individual will of the people for their own good.

A. Challenging the Majority Through Constitutional Limitations.

21 Pettit (1997), page 65.

In order to effectively control state power, according to republican theory, the state must have in place sufficient constitutional restraints that are designed to (1) give the people power against the state ("reciprocal power") to balance the power that the state has over the people, and, more importantly (2) limit the power that the state can exercise.[22] Pettit recognizes the inherent difficulties in a system of creating reciprocal power (whereby the state and the individuals in the state have approximately equal power), and therefore, I will focus primarily on the use of constitutional constraints to limit the state's power to act.[23]

In order for the constitution to properly restrict the modes of state action, it must make those modes (and by "modes" I will assume the constitution itself as well as positive laws) difficult to change. The fact that the law and constitution should remain stable and constant has been recognized for many years,[24] and republican theory holds that the instrumentalities of the state should not be deployed on an arbitrary basis – state actors should not have unfettered discretion in how such instrumentalities are used.[25] Pettit proposes three conditions to prevent this from occurring: (1) the state should be "an empire of laws, not of men,"[26] (2) state power should not be concentrated all in the same body, but rather dispersed among different chambers of the government, and finally (3) there should be in place positive counter-majoritarian protections.[27]

The "empire of laws" condition states that the government should be controlled by the positive law, and not by the ad hoc, random, or arbitrary decisions of the state actors.[28] Essentially, the "empire of laws" condition relates to those characteristics of law that the law must possess to even be rightly considered "law" as such – as in Fuller's eight ways to fail to make law, or Hart's concept of the Rule of Recognition.[29] To be an "empire of laws," a system of positive laws must be enacted which have certain characteristics or attributes, and then the government officials and citizens must then assume that all enacted law in fact possesses these characteristics.[30] Thus, official state decisions should, where possible, be made according to these properly enacted

---

22 Pettit (1997), page 67.
23 Pettit (1997), page 95.
24 See, e.g., Fuller (1969), *The Morality of Law*, rev. ed. New Haven: Yale University Press. Pages 79-81.
25 Pettit (1997), page 173.
26 Pettit, like many others before him, borrows this concept from James Harrington's *The Commonwealth of Oceana* (1656).
27 Pettit (1997), page 173.
28 Pettit (1997), page 174.
29 *Id*; Fuller (1969); H.L.A. Hart, *The Concept of Law*. Oxford: Oxford University Press (1961).
30 Pettit (1997), page 174.

and structured laws, and not according to the individual discretion of the state actor.

Secondly, in order to make the instrumentalities of state action more stable and less changeable, there must be a dispersion of powers. Pettit borrows Montesquieu's tripartite classification and argues that government power should be divided among a legislature, administration, and judiciary.[31] Dispersal of power is necessary because as the power of the state becomes more concentrated in the hands of a few state actors, or groups, there is a greater chance of arbitrary manipulation of the law and a tyranny over the people.[32]

Finally, in addition to creating an empire of laws and dispersing the power among different houses of government, modern republican theory calls for explicit counter-majoritarian enactments, such as a Bill of Rights, that will protect all people from oppression, despite what a majority may enact.[33] The belief in counter-majoritarian protections requires a jurisprudence under which "good law" (not just law) is identified by some criterion other than majority support. For republicanism, this criterion is freedom as non-domination. "'Good law' is law that promotes overall non-domination: law that reduces the domination to which *dominium* may lead without introducing the domination that can do with *imperium*."[34] Thus, the ultimate counter-majoritarian criterion of "good law" is non-domination – law that minimizes individual domination without introducing the type of domination that can control and dominate the entire population. It appears that this may lead to a contradiction – if the majority enacts a law, and that law must then be checked against the ultimate counter-majoritarian condition of promoting overall non-domination, then how do we define "overall non-domination" without referring back to the majority that enacted the law?

B. Challenging the Majority by Giving All People the Power of Contestability.

Separate and apart from the constitutional limitations, Pettit introduces a protection he terms "contestability" because of the possibility that the constitutional limitations still leave too much discretionary power in the hands of judges, administrators, and legislators.[35] "Contestability" is when the person to be interfered with can effectively contest such interference, i.e., make it

[31] Pettit (1997), page 177.
[32] *Id.*
[33] Pettit (1997), page 180.
[34] Pettit (1997), page 182.
[35] Pettit (1997), page 183.

account to his or her relevant interests and ideas.[36] Effective contestability should create a situation of non-arbitrary interference, and thus removes domination.[37]

For contestability to be effective, three conditions must be satisfied. First, decision-making must be done in such a way that there is a potential basis for contesting decisions. The government system of making decisions (of creating laws, rules, etc.) must be structured in such a way as to allow the people to contest the decision (or law or rule). Pettit proposes a deliberative democracy system, where the people are free to debate the relevant issues (instead of instituting a *quid pro quo* deal-making system). Democratic governments promote contestability, and the ability to contest government decisions is a hallmark of democracy.[38]

Secondly, there must be a channel or voice by which contesting decisions can be accomplished. Pettit calls this "inclusiveness" in that everyone who may have a grievance is included in the mechanism to voice that grievance. Inclusiveness is easily established in the legislature in a democracy because legislators are elected by the people (leaving aside the issue that legislators are only elected by a majority of their constituents). However, inclusiveness is harder to establish in the administration and the judiciary. Pettit proposes a proportional representation system – as in a jury-like cross section of society – whereby the administration and judiciary are comprised of the demographic make up of society. "Let the administration or the judiciary become statistically unrepresentative of major stakeholders and there is no longer a guarantee that members of unrepresented groups can make their voices heard in appropriate circles."[39]

Thirdly, there must be a suitable forum in existence for hearing contestations, a forum where the validity of the claim is assessed and a suitable response is determined.[40] This "suitable forum" is the "responsive republic" where the people are guaranteed that the grievances they make will receive a proper hearing. However, there may be at least two reasons why a person's grievance would not be properly heard (1) the person is guided by self-interest, and thus the judgment is made that the common interest requires frustration of that

---

[36] Pettit (1997), page 184.
[37] *Id.*
[38] Pettit (1997), page 185.
[39] Pettit (1997), pages 192-193.
[40] Pettit (1997), page 186.

person's interests, or (2) the contestation may represent the minority's judgment of what is in the common interest.[41]

Clearly, there is an inherent contradiction in stating that everyone's grievances must be heard, and then stating that it would be an acceptable reason not to address a person's grievance because it may be part of the minority position. How should a non-dominating government respond to the minority? "At the limit, the ideal of non-domination may require in relevant cases that the group are allowed to secede from the state, establishing a separate territory or at least a separate jurisdiction; that possibility has to be firmly on the horizon."[42] Short of outright succession, the state should have some method of conscientious procedural objection.[43] However, in his later work, Pettit backs off this position substantially: "I shall assume that it cannot feasibly exempt unwilling members from its laws, dealing in a different way with those in the territory who identify sufficiently to endorse membership, and those who don't. And I shall assume that, consistently with caring about freedom as non-domination, it cannot give special privileges to those who seek such a status; this would mean that the privileged were well placed to dominate the underprivileged."[44]

If the law is to be both coercive and non-dominating, it must be created under the collective control of the people. No one can be left out from the process – all members must share in the collective control.[45] In other words, the people should identify a good or public interest, "avowed in common by all," and then create procedures where that interest would dictate the policies to be put in place.[46] Pettit proposes this "convergence method" to establishing and implementing the common interest: (1) there are public-goods policies in any domain such that everyone would prefer that one of them be collectively and coercively implemented to nothing's being done by the government; (2) only a proper subset of public-goods policies will satisfy the constraint of mutually acceptable reasons in any domain and, special interests aside, everyone would prefer that one of those policies should be implemented there rather than one of the policies that fail it; and (3) only a certain number of procedures for choosing between remaining policies will satisfy the constraint of mutually acceptable reasons and, special interests aside, everyone would prefer that one such procedure be established – on a similarly acceptable basis – and that a

[41] Pettit (1997), page 198.
[42] Pettit (1997), page 199.
[43] *Id.*
[44] Pettit (2008).
[45] *Id.* Inexplicably, Pettit states that this mechanism also respects the view that opening power to the people does not mean a tyranny of the majority.
[46] *Id.*

policy that is selected by that procedure should be implemented rather than any alternative.[47] If there then exist a number of different policies that are consistent with mutually acceptable reasons, but one procedure suits one faction and one suits another, then Pettit states there should be some tiebreaker, like a lottery.[48]

The public interest has to be defined on the basis of democratic discussion and contestation amongst the people and so that it requires institutions that make room for the debate processes.[49] Given the public interest and public role in making the laws, are the laws then non-dominating? "Let the public interest rule, and we let an interest rule in which each member of an equally inclusive, contestatory democracy is invested; it is an interest implicit, after all, in the way that discussion and contestation is conducted amongst its members. Let the public interest rule, then, and we let the public rule."[50]

C. Problem #2 – Constitutional Limits and Contestability Do Not Effectively Control the Tyranny of the Majority.

1. Constitutional Problems.

Constitutional limits, like laws, represent interference over the people to perform certain activities. Therefore, in order to not infringe on freedom, the constitutional limitations themselves, like laws, must not be arbitrary and dominating. Since arbitrariness is determined by considering the needs and wants of the people over whom the interference will be in effect, the arbitrariness of constitutional limitations must be examined in comparison to the needs and wants of the people as a whole. This leads to a situation where the state is creating constitutional limitations to control state power in the very same manner that will lead to arbitrariness and domination of the law. To ensure that the constitutional limitations themselves, as well as the laws they are created to limit, are non-dominating, state actors must consider the needs and wants of the people. And since they cannot consider the needs and wants of each individual person, as shown in Problem #1 above, they must consider the needs and wants of the people as a group. And since, as a group, the people will have diverse needs and wants, the concerns of the majority will take precedence. In creating constitutional limitations to protect against the tyranny of the majority, the state can only go back to that same tyrannical majority to ensure that the constitution itself is not the source of domination.

---

47 *Id.*
48 *Id.*
49 *Id.*
50 *Id.*

I do not take issue with Pettit's arguments that the state should be an "empire of laws and not of men" and the state power should be dispersed among different houses of government. Generally speaking, in the abstract at least, Pettit's last category of constitutional limitation should also be acceptable. In order to protect against majority domination of the minority, the constitution itself must include express counter-majoritarian restrictions. A ready example of this is the Bill of Rights to the United States Constitution, which provides protections of the freedom of speech, freedom of assembly, and against the establishment of religion. No law can be created which violates one of these, or any, constitutional provisions, or it will risk being struck by the chief arbiter of constitutional interpretation – the United States Supreme Court.

However, the argument for counter-majoritarian conditions in the constitution brings us back to the majority itself. The constitution must provide some criterion (or, presumably, criteria) against which a "good law" can be measured as valid without resorting to the fact that it has majority support. This criterion must promote overall non-domination. Unfortunately, "non-domination" is defined with reference to whether the law is arbitrary, which itself is then defined as whether the law takes into account the people's opinions, wants and desires. And with one more step – the step that it is the majority's opinions, wants and desires that are taken into account in a diverse society – we find ourselves back at the tyranny of the majority. Counter-majoritarian conditions must validate the law based on something other than majority rule, and that "something" must be the overall non-domination that the law entails, which then itself must refer back to majority rule to determine whether it is either "overall" or "dominating/arbitrary."

In any common view of liberty, it is readily conceivable that the constitution must contain some absolute protections against certain acts of the majority – so-called counter-majoritarian conditions. However, this idea is probably better explained, in such a view, by vague reference to a Bill of Rights than it is by trying to relate it to republicanism's overall argument of non-domination. It is not a given fact that majority domination can be controlled, even in a democratic republic like the United States. To have a chance of controlling the majority's ability to pass laws that dominate over the minority, the constitution must contain absolutes that are unchangeable, or nearly so. How do we come by such absolute inviolable principles? Do we turn to religion? To ideology? To the mandates of Mill's utilitarianism or Kant's deontological ethics?

The only way to counter the majority is to eliminate it, abstractly, in determining what counter-majoritarian principles must be in the constitution. For example, if 60% of the population of a new state were of ideology A, and

20% were of ideology B, and 10% were of ideology C, and the remaining 10% were of ideologies D through Z, then perhaps one member of each ideology is chosen to represent it at a constitutional convention where the counter-majoritarian principles are drafted. Or, more realistically, one member from each of the ideologies comprising a super-majority of the population, say 80 or 90%, would be present. Each would get one vote on certain fundamental rights, freedoms, or protections to be enacted. With only one vote per group, there is no "tyranny of the majority" that can design a constitution to give legitimacy to dominating acts of the majority, but rather, the majority would have no more say in what is part of the constitution than even a small minority.

2. Contestability Problems.

The bigger problem for republicanism is not the constitutional limitations, but the concept of contestability. By allowing the people to have the ability to contest government action, the state will not abuse its power (or at least such abuses will be minimized). However, once this concept is deconstructed into its component parts, it quickly unravels.

First, the theory holds, the state's decision-making procedures must be structured in such a way as to allow a citizen to contest the decision – the deliberative democracy. This should allow decisions of the state to be debated in an open forum, and then ultimately subjected to the majority vote of the democracy (whether directly by the population, or by elected representatives). While I agree that free and open debate is an important part of protecting the population against impingements of their freedom, the fact that this prong of "contestability" refers back to majority vote undermines the very protection it is intended to give. Perhaps the citizen can contest a particular decision if they happen to fall into the majority, but for those in the minority, their contest is ineffective.

Second, the element of "inclusiveness" requires that the mechanism by which grievances are heard include everyone in society. For each person to be properly heard, they must be properly represented in the mechanism of government. This is easily accomplished in the democratic legislature, where each representative is voted in by the population (leaving aside the problem with majority rule voting). However, it is not clear how a proportional demographic representation in the administration or judiciary can lead to some higher (or better) level of contestability. While I agree that in the abstract, the ability to contest (or voice an opposition to) state action should be possessed by everyone in the population, I do not agree that this is best accomplished in a manner where the population must rely on (1) majority rule and (2) vague demographic criteria for representation. How would this work in the administration or judiciary? What are the relevant factors to take into account? Race, religion, education, social status, wealth, age, sex, sexual orientation? Is there a hierarchy of factors, or should all of these be ranked equally? How often should the population undergo a census in order to ensure proportional representation in these bodies of government? Should some factors, like education, be excluded entirely, as in the case of the judiciary (assuming that the judiciary should not be representative of both the most and least intelligent in society)?

Furthermore, the concept of proportional representation is not logically related to the ability to contest government action. This basis for contestability assumes that by having an administration and judiciary that are the same demographic make-up of society, that the society's interests will be better represented. There is some logical traction in the idea that, again in the abstract, a government that looks like the people will better represent the people. However, am I more adequately represented in government because I am a Catholic, and therefore the Catholic members of the judiciary and administration share my views on certain issues? If I'm African-American, can I assume that any African-American in the administration or judiciary will represent my interests? This view neglects the complex and multi-faceted nature of one's political and social beliefs and instead focuses on factors that are tangentially related, if at all, to one's views.

The final prong of contestability is that a forum must exist where the people can be assured that their grievance will receive a proper hearing, or the "responsive republic." This element of contestability is qualified with two large exceptions to the rule of "responsiveness" that eviscerate its effectiveness. The first major exception is that if a person is guided by individual self interest, the judgment can be made that the common interest requires frustration of that party's wishes. If it is determined that the person voicing the grievance is acting not in the common interest, but rather self-interest, then the person's grievance need not be heard, or rather heard and disregarded. The majority would be determining the "common interest" and thus, anything that does not match the common interest can be classified as individual self-interest and disregarded. The second major exception to the final prong of contestability is merely the first exception, but stated more boldly: the grievance simply represents the minority interest, and therefore can be excluded.

Contestability is a sham protection. Giving people the right to contest government action, even through a well-run judicial process, does not guarantee that the contesting citizen will be successful. Furthermore, what if the state decides that certain forms of contestability, such as a free press, or demonstrations, are not for the betterment of the people and not in their best interests? The state can do away with these for the citizenry's own good, and still not reduce freedom. The limits and effect of contestability, short of the threat of civil war, are completely within the control of the state and the majority of citizens that support the state. As a single person fighting against the passage of a law that I consider particularly oppressive, is my freedom any better protected whether I am fighting the fight alone, or with ten friends, or with 49% of the entire state? In all of those scenarios, I lose, and I am subject to interference against my will.

It is not completely fair to fault Pettit for failing to establish protections against majority domination that are not themselves based on the will of the majority. In a democratic system, where the people vote on the constitutional amendments or (directly or indirectly) for the laws, majority rule is the only way to achieve an acceptable outcome. However, this failing must be widely acknowledged and understood, and not hidden in the context of counter-majoritarian conditions. Certainly, it must not be disguised as protection for the people.

III. Relativistic Freedom and the Problem of International Power.

A. Freedom on a Global Scale.

Essentially, the concept of freedom from the republican camp is not confined to geographic borders, and it can be examined on an international scale. If the state is not adequately secured and protected, there is a constant threat of domination from external agents – other more powerful countries.[51] In the threat of external domination, the best answer is not going to be immediate violence, but rather a "readying" of the state for potential conflict through the building up of armies and arms.[52] Pettit analogizes this readying for conflict to the concept of "reciprocal power" he described with reference to the limits on the state's power and also argues that the situation may be better resolved through being a "good international citizen" and supporting a body like the United Nations.[53] In other words, a state should support other states with constitutional constraints on power and promote this as an international goal with other states and through the United Nations.[54]

---

[51] Pettit (1997), page 150.
[52] Pettit (1997), page 151.
[53] Pettit (1997), page 152.
[54] *Id.*

In his zeal to promote multinational cooperation and "good international citizenship," Pettit argues for a weakening of state sovereignty and a turning over of certain historically domestic issues to international decision-making and adjudication, such as homosexuality and gay rights, development in a certain wilderness area, and women's rights. "[International bodies] may promise to do better in the promotion of freedom as non-domination among the citizens of that state than the state itself. The best republican policy may well be to expatriate domestic sovereignty in such cases and to give a certain guaranteed weight, if not absolute discretion, to relevant international agencies."[55]

B. Problem #3 – Freedom is Always Relative.

Assuming that Pettit's republican freedom can be set up in a state such that only non-arbitrary interference is imposed on the people, Pettit himself admits that freedom and domination are relative. Freedom, under the republican theory, is when people are not subjected to the arbitrary interference from another person or collective of people, or even the potential for such arbitrary interference. Assume for the sake of argument that through properly considering the people's needs and wants, and instituting such power-abuse controls as constitutional limitations, and contestability, there is no possibility of arbitrary interference and the people in a given state can consider themselves "free."

However, this freedom is relative only to their own state and time. They are not free throughout all time and space, but free with respect to a particular time in history with respect to a particular government, their own, for sure, and perhaps with respect to some other non-threatening governments. I am in State A, a large powerful state with high GDP, a stable democratic government, and strong military. Assuming all of the factors above, the world will look at the citizenry of State A generally as "free" or possessing many "freedoms." State B is smaller, has a smaller population, smaller military, smaller GDP, but possesses the same safeguards above, and therefore its citizenry is considered "free" from arbitrary rule by the government of State B. Is State B really "free?" Even if unlikely to happen, isn't there the chance of invasion and arbitrary control over B by State A? Even if State A is a "benevolent master", doesn't State B only enjoy its freedoms at the pleasure of State A?

Consider States C, D, and E. All of these states are smaller, with smaller populations, maybe with governments not as stable as A or B, but they do have some military force. And they hate State A for ideological reasons.

[55] Pettit (1997), page 153.

Individually, State A could dominate any of those states, and could probably even dominate a number of combinations of those states. But it is clear that if States B, C, D, E, and maybe others, joined forces against A, they would dominate State A and impose their arbitrary rule over the citizens of State A. This is a possibility, however remote. Are the citizens of State A really "free"? Are they mostly "free"? Are they "free" to a probability of 95%?

Unless there is one state that can effectively defend itself against an onslaught of attack from the rest of the world, and thus runs no potentiality of being dominated by any combination of other states, there is no freedom as non-domination in the world from the republican perspective.

IV. Conclusions.

In this brief account of the republican ideal of freedom, I have attempted to set out the main tenants of that ideal, at least as described by one of its contemporary scholars, Philip Pettit. According to this account of freedom, we see law as an oppressive, but necessary force that has the potential of reducing freedom of a society. We need law to structure government and restrain people's actions, but how is that accomplished without imposing a harsh, totalitarian regime?

In the republican theory, freedom is only harmed by "domination" that comes as a result of "arbitrary" laws or interference. Laws are arbitrary to the extent that they do not account for the opinions and desires of those on whom they are imposed. And how is it determined that laws do take this into account, and are thus non-arbitrary? Either the ruling autocrat dictates the law, claiming to have taken these issues into account, or the people themselves (directly or through democratic representation) vote for the laws on a majority basis. Republicans recognize the inherent problem of the "tyranny of the majority" and to combat that, Pettit argues for restrictions on power, coming in the form of (1) constitutional constraints on the government and (2) giving the people the power to contest those decisions.

Despite these arguments, republicans cannot account for two major sources of oppression of freedom (1) the state's ability to legislate for the people's own good over their objection, in a Hegelian sense, and (2) the tyranny of the majority. Pettit institutes several mechanisms designed to combat the majority rule, should it oppress the minority, even going so far as to label one such restriction "counter-majoritarian conditions." None of it will logically protect the citizens against the majority, however.

First, by bifurcating the needs and wants of the state into individual versus community needs and goals, the ruling party can easily create laws that take into account the necessary conditions to be labeled "non-arbitrary" and hence "non-dominating" by merely claiming that such laws are created for the good of the people, as a whole, by legislators that have their best interests at heart. Any dissention from this could easily be labeled as the selfish view of a minority, or worse, the selfish view of individuals as to their individual interest, which is always subordinated to the group or community interest.

Secondly, the constitutional and contestatory "restrictions" on oppressive state action still rely on majority rule in some fashion or another. The constitution is created by majority rule or by rulers chosen by some other means who will act without input of the people (the definition of "arbitrary"). The ability of citizens to effectively contest state decisions would protect them from arbitrary state power, but the principals of contestability are not workable from the republican standpoint. It requires us to create a system that allows citizens the ability to contest decisions, and it requires the government to represent the demographic makeup of the people, or be chosen by the people. Legislators are elected, but the judiciary and administration are not, so they should be chosen to represent a slice of society. Even if this can be readily accomplished (and it cannot) the fact that a citizen shares some characteristic with a person in the state government does not mean that such state actor will protect, or even share, the citizen's concerns.

Finally, under this republican outlook, there is no ultimate freedom, only degrees of freedom of one party relative to another. It is not clear whether there are any criteria, in a concrete sense, so claim that the people of a certain state are "free" or not. But worse for this theory, even if the people can claim to be free in their state, they may not be free from the exercise (or the threat of exercise) of arbitrary power from a neighboring state. At this point in history, it would be difficult to imagine that the people of the United States are free from domination and oppression from the United States (or any of the several states) government, but not free from the potential of arbitrary rule of neighbors like Mexico or Canada. However, in 1991, the people of Kuwait could have been considered "free" from oppressive rule by their own government, but certainly subject to the arbitrary rule of neighboring Iraq. Clearly other power dynamics have existed and continue to exist around the world – the U.S. and the U.S.S.R. during the Cold War era, India and Pakistan, Israel and Iran, and the list could continue on. The republican theory has missed the mark. At best, it does not provide a more workable theory of freedom for states to implement, and at worst, it provides states an easier mechanism to dominate the people.

Made in the USA
Monee, IL
05 November 2026

67814354R00049